MEN-AT-ARMS SERIES

EDITOR: MARTIN WINDROW

# New Model Army
## 1645-60

*Text by* STUART ASQUITH

*Colour plates by* CHRIS WARNER

OSPREY PUBLISHING LONDON

Published in 1981 by
Osprey Publishing Ltd
Member company of the George Philip Group
12–14 Long Acre, London WC2E 9LP
© Copyright 1981 Osprey Publishing Ltd

ISBN 0 85045 385 2

Filmset in Great Britain
Printed in Singapore through
Graphic Consultants International Pte Ltd

Among those who have earned the grateful thanks of
the author and illustrator for their patient help and
advice during the preparation of this book we would
particularly like to thank Mr A. V. B. Norman of the
Tower Armouries, and his photographic librarian
Mr Roger Freeman; Gerry Embleton; Miss Avril
Hart of the Victoria and Albert Museum; Charles
Kightley; and Mr D. S. Wills of Littlecote House,
near Hungerford, Berkshire, where many surviving
examples of period equipment may be seen, on
display throughout the year.

This book is for Karen, Rachel and Thomas

## Select Bibliography

Ashley, Maurice, *The English Civil War*, 1974
Ashley, Maurice, *Cromwell and his World*, 1972
Asquith, Stuart, *The Campaign of Naseby*, 1979
Cunnington, *English Costume in the 17th Century*, 1955
Elton, Richard, *The Compleat Body of the Art Military*, 1650
Firth, C. H., *Cromwell's Army*, 1962
Firth, C. H., *Regimental History of Cromwell's Army*, 1940
Fortescue, Sir John, *History of the British Army*, Vol. 1, 1899
Grose, George, *Military Antiquities*
Kellie, Sir Thomas, in *Pallas Armata*, 1627
Kelly and Schwabe, *A Short History of Costume and Armour*, 1931
Le Blond, Guillaume, *A Treatise of Artillery*, 1970
Manucy, Albert, *Artillery Through the Ages*, 1949
Orrery, Roger Earl of, *A Treatise on the Art of War*, 1677
Petersen, H. L., *Roundshot and Rammers*, 1969
Potter, R. and Embleton, G. A., *The English Civil War*, 1973
Reed, W., *Lore of Arms*, 1976
Turner, Sir James, in *Pallas Armata*, 1671
Waugh, Nora, *The Cut of Men's Clothes*, 1964
Wagner, E., *Swords and Daggers*, 1975
Wedgewood, C. V., *Milton and his World*, 1969
Wilkinson, F., *Antique Arms and Armour*, 1972
Young, P., *English Civil War Armies*, 1973

*Standards Taken in the Civil War* (contemp.)
*The Compleat Gunner*, 1672 (S. R. Publishers, 1971)

# *Introduction*

Many authorities quote the Restoration of 1660 as the birth date of our modern British Army. While this may be true as far as continuity of unit identity is concerned, it is untrue in a far more fundamental sense. The evidence of history shows that the creation of an efficient military machine, and its proving on the battlefield, predates the Restoration by 15 years. It was on the fields of Naseby, Dunbar and the Dunes that the foundations of the British professional army were laid.

While this book deals primarily with the New Model Army from its formation in 1645 until the Restoration, it is inevitable that other aspects of 17th century society are mentioned. To talk of the New Model is to talk of Oliver Cromwell; and to talk of Cromwell is to talk of politics. In the mid-17th century the army was a much more powerful force, relatively speaking, than it is today, both in its monopoly of physical power and in its political influence. In the absence of any type of civil police the army ruled, and represented what law and order there was. To be a senior commander was automatically to wield political power. On more than one occasion generals marched their men down to a Parliament with which they disagreed, and either expelled selected Honourable Members, or closed the House down altogether. The New Model owed its birth to what was essentially a political decision.

## The Origins of the New Model

Sir William Waller (1597–1668), son of a Lieutenant of Dover Castle, was one of the first Parliamentary leaders to take the field. He saw successful action at the end of 1642 in Dorset, Hampshire and Sussex: and as a direct result Parliament placed him in command of the army of the Western Association (Gloucestershire, Wiltshire, Somerset, Worcester, Shropshire and the city of Bristol) upon its formation on 11 February 1643. When this army was largely destroyed at the fateful battle of Roundway Down (13 July 1643), Waller moved on to take command of the South Eastern Association army (Kent, Surrey, Sussex and Hampshire) from its beginnings in early November 1643. Since his forces now consisted of both Association troops and those of the London Trained Bands, Waller had great difficulty in keeping his army

Sir Thomas Fairfax, later 3rd Baron Fairfax of Cameron (1612–71), chosen by Parliament to command the New Model upon its formation, and architect of the new army; under his hand the different elements began to cohere into a professionally trained and led force. Replaced by Cromwell when he refused to lead the army against the Scots in 1650, he played no further part in public life, but lent his support to George Monck's preparations for the Restoration. (National Army Museum)

intact in the field. The London regiments—by far the strongest available to Parliament—would only serve for short periods, and were not to be relied upon for service in lengthy campaigns. The commercial life of the city virtually came to a standstill when the Trained Bands marched out of London; and those who held the purse-strings were constantly pressing for their early return.

An ordinance passed in March 1644 went some way towards stabilizing the fluctuating strength of Waller's forces, by providing for the raising of an army for him which would serve more permanently and in sufficient strength to counter the Royal army. Waller's new army saw action at Cropredy Bridge (28 June 1644) and at the second battle of Newbury (27 October 1644). At Second Newbury Waller's forces outnumbered those of the king two to one, yet were still unable to force a decision. This experience, coupled with his unhappy memories of local armies which fought bravely to defend their own country but would not move outside it, must have crystallized Waller's belief that the war could never be won until Parliament had an army which could be relied upon to serve when, where, and for however long the military situation dictated. Waller's views were widely shared among senior Parliamentary officers, and events came to a head in December 1644 when Oliver Cromwell made a major speech calling for a remedy to Parliament's military failings.

Much debate followed, but as a direct result of Cromwell's speech the formation of the New Model Army was sanctioned on 4 February 1645. The Self-Denying Ordinance, which was passed by Parliament on 3 April 1645, forbade members of either House from holding military rank or office. This vital reform swept away much of the 'dead wood' from the hierarchy of Parliament's armies, leaving the field clear for the professional soldiers—such as were available. Ironically enough it also swept away Waller himself—but

The steel head of a Civil War pike, showing the metal tongues down the ash shaft which prevented the point being lopped off by enemy horsemen. (NAM)

with him went other and far less able men. The new army was formed under the command of Sir Thomas Fairfax (1612–71), an experienced soldier of courage, intelligence and integrity.

# Organization

The New Model was formed from three Parliamentary armies: those of the Eastern Association, led by the Earl of Manchester, Sir William Waller, and the Earl of Essex. In its original form it had 12 regiments of foot, 11 of horse, one of dragoons, and two companies of 'firelocks' (see under Artillery). Each regiment was identified by the name of its colonel, and those in office on the formation of the New Model were as follows:

| Regiment of Foot | Army of Origin |
| --- | --- |
| Sir Thomas Fairfax | Essex and Eastern Assoc. |
| Colonel Fortescue | Essex |
| Colonel Robert Hammond | Eastern Assoc. |
| Colonel Edward Harley | Essex |
| Colonel Richard Ingoldsby | Essex |
| Colonel Walter Lloyd | Essex |
| Colonel Edward Montagu | Eastern Assoc. |
| Colonel John Pickering | Eastern Assoc. |
| Colonel Thomas Rainsborough | Eastern Assoc. |
| Sir Philip Skippon | Essex |
| Sir Hardress Waller | Waller |
| Colonel Ralph Weldon | Waller |

| Regiment of Horse | |
| --- | --- |
| Sir Thomas Fairfax (Col. John Butler O/C) | Eastern Assoc. |
| Colonel John Butler | Waller |
| Colonel Fleetwood | Eastern Assoc. |
| Earl of Essex (Col. Richard Graves O/C) | Essex |
| Colonel Henry Ireton | Waller |
| Colonel Robert Pye | Waller |
| Colonel Nathaniel Rich | Eastern Assoc. |
| Colonel Edward Rossiter | Eastern Assoc. |
| Colonel James Sheffield | Essex |
| Colonel Vermuyden | Eastern Assoc. |
| Colonel Edward Whalley | Eastern Assoc. |

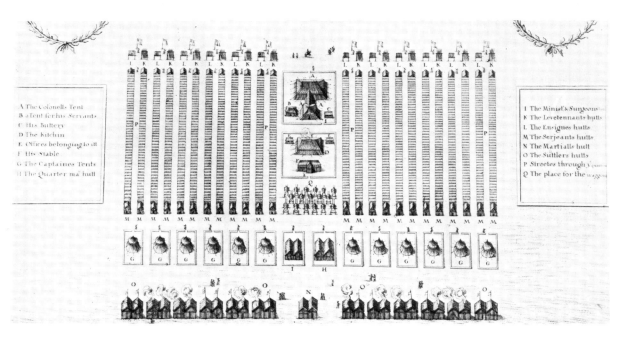

The policy adopted throughout this book is to refer to a regiment by the name of its *original colonel*. To emphasize the wisdom of this convention, one need do no more than describe in brief detail the career of a single regiment of foot—that of Sir Thomas Fairfax.

Formed from a cadre based on Fairfax's regiment in the army of the Earl of Essex, and commanded by Lieutenant-Colonel Jackson, the 'new' Fairfax's Regiment was established on 18 March 1645. After sterling service at Naseby, Torrington and Wallingford the officers of the regiment were caught up in the 'great unrest' and were summarily replaced. The new lieutenant-colonel was William Cawell, formerly a major in Harley's Regiment; when he was mortally wounded at Preston in 1648 he was replaced in his turn by one Goffe, from the same regiment, one of the signatories of the king's death warrant. Goffe led Fairfax's Regiment at the battle of Dunbar, the colonel now being Cromwell, since Fairfax had declined to take any part in the invasion of Scotland. The regiment fought well, and Goffe became a full colonel; he was confirmed by Parliament in his appointment as lieutenant-colonel of the regiment, an event perhaps not wholly unconnected with the fact that it was his major who carried the news of victory, and more than 150 captured enemy colours, to Parliament. The regiment served at Worcester in 1651, and as

**A contemporary illustration depicting the ideal regimental infantry camp in the field; we may doubt that such perfect order was often achieved even in the later years of the New Model. The colonel's marquee is in the centre flanked by rows of 'rank and file' accommodation. The junior officers' quarters are across the top, and those of more senior officers across the bottom; below these, outside the confines of the camp, are the sutlers' huts. (NAM)**

marines in the Dutch War. Political intrigue now took a hand; in 1659 the newly-restored Long Parliament cashiered Goffe and replaced him temporarily with Ludlow. On Ludlow's appointment as commander-in-chief in Ireland the colonelcy was taken over by Herbert Morley. Morley was the last officer to hold it; on 15 November 1660, at Reading, the regiment was disbanded and paid off.

This confusing succession of six commanders, and thus six contemporarily used names within a period of 15 years, is entirely typical of the New Model, and explains why for clarity this book will use the name of the original commander throughout. For the record, the names of subsequent commanders of the other foot regiments were as follows; note that name-spellings were by no means rigidly constant:

| | |
|---|---|
| *Fortescue's:* | Barkstead, Fitch, Miller, Twisleton, Massey |
| *Hammond's:* | Ewer, Lawrence |
| *Harley's:* | Pride, Moss |
| *Ingoldsby's:* | Mill, Sydenham, Lenthall, Earl of Northampton |

Oliver Cromwell (1599–1658)—the famous portrait by Walker shows the creator of the Ironsides at the age of 50 in 1649, on the eve of the Scottish expedition. A born soldier of humble origins, Cromwell's military record in the Civil Wars was second to none. His 'reign' as Lord Protector from 1653 to 1658 has marked him for later generations as either a visionary political figure or a loathsome tyrant, and both cases are equally arguable; his religious bigotry, and the bitter fruit it bore in Ireland, are sadly beyond dispute. He remains secure in his reputation as one of the most extraordinary Englishmen who ever lived. (National Portrait Gallery)

| | |
|---|---|
| *Lloyd's:* | Herbert, Overton, Fenwick, Wilkes, Hughes |
| *Montagu's:* | Lambert, Constable, Biscoe, Fleetwood, Cholmley |
| *Pickering's:* | Hewson, Streeter, Lord Bellasis |
| *Rainsborough's:* (*Rainsborowe's*) | Deane |
| *Skippon's:* | Sydenham, Coxe, Ashfield |
| *Weldon's:* | Lilburne, Hesilrige |

The regiments of horse were subject to a similar succession of commanders. That of Colonel Nathaniel Rich provides a typical example.

In 1644 Rich had been lieutenant-colonel of the Earl of Manchester's own regiment of horse in the Eastern Association army, and took many of the troopers into his newly formed New Model regiment. After service at Naseby, the storming of Bristol and the blockade of Oxford, the regiment opposed Parliament's plans to disband it in 1647, being caught up like Fairfax's Foot in the 'great unrest'. Ironically, Rich's were detailed for the protection of Parliament, and were quartered in the Royal Mews. They were active again in May 1648, putting down a number of Royalist adventures in Kent and the south-east at the insistence of Parliament. Rich's regiment was not granted permission to join Cromwell, and was once more detailed for the defence of the House of Commons; but in July 1651 they marched north, and saw action at Warrington and Worcester.

In December 1654 Colonel Rich was arrested for anti-government activities, being released and then re-arrested in 1656. In the meantime, in January 1655, he was replaced as colonel by Charles Howard, the Governor of Carlisle. In September of that year command passed to Richard Ingoldsby, but he does not seem to have actually joined the regiment, which was then in Scotland. In May 1659 the recalled Long Parliament replaced Ingoldsby with Colonel Okey; in June 1659 the political ferment of the day brought Nathaniel Rich back to replace Okey; and in February 1660 Ingoldsby returned for his second term as colonel. The last action before the Restoration was the suppression of a rising near Daventry in April 1660; and the regiment was finally disbanded on 5 December that year.

The full list of colonels of the other cavalry regiments was as follows:

| | |
|---|---|
| *Fairfax's:* | Cromwell, Richard Cromwell, Packer, Hesilrige, Fauconbridge, Duke of York |
| *Butler's:* | Horton, Sankey |
| *Fleetwood's:* | Cooper |
| *Graves's:* | Scroope |
| *Ireton's:* | Fleetwood, Cooper, Markham |
| *Pye's:* | Tomlinson, Monck |
| *Rossiter's:* | Twisleton, Clobery |
| *Sheffield's:* | Harrison, Winthrop, Montague, Alured, Montagu |
| *Vermuyden's:* | Cromwell, Disbrowe, Walton |
| *Whalley's:* | Swallow, Saunders, Lord Falkland |

The New Model did not absorb all the Parliamentary units in the field immediately upon its formation. Major-General Poyntz had a sizeable force in the north of England, as did Major-General Massey in the West Country. There was a Midlands army of levies under Major-General Browne, and smaller numbers of troops scattered in Wales. Most of these units did gradually join the New Model; at Dunbar in 1650 we find regiments formerly of Poyntz's command serving in the main order of battle.

The New Model grew in size from its original 24 regiments to a total of about 100, but it was a gradual process. Early in 1649 just over 44,000 men were under arms for Parliament, while in mid-1652 the figure was around 68,000. In fact 1652 was the high-water mark of Parliamentarian strength; 1654 found the total down to just under 53,000, and at the Restoration there were little over 28,000.

## Regimental Establishment: The Foot

On its formation in 1645 the regiments of the New Model were organized on the basis of the existing units from which they originated. There were gradual changes due to alterations to establishment, reflecting a constant lack of manpower. Initially a regiment of New Model infantry would have 1,200 men at full establishment. These were organized in ten unequally sized companies: the colonel's company had 200 men, the lieutenant-colonel's 160, the sergeant-major's 140, and each of the seven captains' companies 100 men. It was rare to see a regiment at full strength, however; 700 was considered a very strong establishment, and 300 to 500 was typical. It was normal for this to be reflected in a reduction in the number of captains' companies, rather than an even reduction in company strength throughout the unit.

The companies were each made up of two-thirds musketeers and one-third pikemen. The company would muster in a six-deep formation, with two bodies of musketeers flanking the pikemen. A further sub-division existed in the file of six men, led by a file leader; the file leaders made up the front rank of the company, and were, presumably, steady and reliable soldiers.

The officers generally comprised a captain in command, a lieutenant as second-in-command, and an ensign who carried the company colour. There were generally three or four sergeants, responsible both for the overall appearance of the company on the march or in the line of battle, and for supplies of match, powder and so forth. Other grades appear to have been present in varying numbers. There was, for example, no fixed ratio of corporals to numbers of men, as they seem to have been appointed at regimental level to suit company needs. Their rôle was not so much

disciplinary—as was the case with sergeants—but more as instructors. It was the corporal who demonstrated to the newly joined recruit the drill with pike and musket.

Also on the strength were two drummers per company, who played an important rôle. All manoeuvring on the field of battle or on the march was controlled by drums, which had eight basic calls. The 'call' passed the order to muster on the company colour, and the 'troop' signalled a ready position. 'Preparative' was the signal to close ranks and adopt fighting stance, and was followed by the 'battle' or 'charge', depending on the circumstances. If things went badly the 'retreat' signalled withdrawal; and the 'march' meant just that. 'Revalley' and 'tattoo' were peaceful camp signals.

The well-organized company was purely an administrative unit however; on the battlefield the regiment would deploy in three bodies, each a larger-size copy of the company deployment, with wings of musketeers flanking a central body of pikes. At both company and regimental level these bodies of men were termed 'divisions', which seem to have had a fairly loose definition. Assuming full regimental strength deployed for battle in three bodies in a six-deep formation, regimental frontage would be something in the region of 250 yards, although this figure probably varied considerably with the irregular establishments mentioned above.

The whole regiment would be commanded by

Henry Ireton (1611–51) fought with Cromwell at Marston Moor and commanded the left wing at Naseby, where he was wounded and captured. After a foray into politics he married Cromwell's daughter Bridget; he was a faithful lieutenant to his father-in-law, and was a signatory of Charles I's death warrant. He died of plague during the Irish campaign; upon the Restoration his grave in Westminster Abbey was desecrated and his remains exhibited on Tyburn gallows. (NPG)

Pikemen, or officers of pikes, from the stained glass windows of Farndon Church. Though depicting Royalist troops at the siege of Chester, they are useful near-contemporary evidence. The corselet and tassets are clearly seen, as is a morion helmet with flowing plumes. The next picture shows a reconstruction apparently based on the left-hand figure; detail and proportions are slightly odd. (NAM)

the lieutenant-colonel: the colonel himself was generally a titular commander only, and was usually a general officer anyway.

The pike was considered a more honourable weapon than the musket, and the regimental colours—one per company—were carried in their ranks when in battle.

Gradually the discrepancy between company strengths seems to have disappeared, but in the mid-1650s the New Model regiments were still formed of uneven companies. Those of the colonel, lieutenant-colonel and sergeant-major had 145 men each, and the remaining seven companies 109 men each, giving an overall theoretical strength of 1,198, plus officers. The term 'officer' is one which was rather loosely applied in the mid-17th century, covering a colonel, a sergeant and even a drummer: in other words, any man who did not muster in the main body of regimental rank and file. Assuming this meaning, the total estab-

lishment would be 1,298, a figure rarely, if ever, achieved.

There are indications that by the time of the Restoration, New Model companies were of equal size and that the establishment norm had become 1,000 men.

**The Dragoons**
The New Model initially had only one regiment of dragoons, commanded by Colonel John Okey. This was 1,000 strong, with ten equally-sized troops of 100 men. The dragoon was a hybrid soldier, a cross between infantryman and trooper, and the company organization in Okey's regiment reflected this. Each company had a captain, a lieutenant, a cornet and a quartermaster—cavalry ranks; but each company also had two drummers for signalling, as in infantry units.

Initially Okey's regiment followed the true dragoon or mounted infantry practice, i.e. they arrived on the field of battle on horseback but dismounted to fight. However, it would appear that they began to function more and more as regular cavalry, and in 1650 they were officially converted into a regiment of horse (receiving thereby substantial pay rises!). The strength and number of companies in a dragoon regiment varied considerably, depending on the task to hand. Morgan's Regiment, for example, raised for service in Scotland in 1651, had in October of that year eight troops—but in January 1653 we find only four troops each of only 60 men. Dragoon units were fairly easily raised, for most counties had companies of militia dragoons. They were particularly useful units for 'police' duties; and it is rare to find all ten companies of Okey's Regiment serving together after the Naseby campaign.

**The Horse**
The basic unit of cavalry was the troop, averaging some 60 troopers but rising occasionally to as many as 80. Generally there were six troops in a regiment, but instances of eight were not uncommon. Cromwell's own regiment of horse, dubbed 'The Ironsides', was a double-strength regiment of 14 troops, and upon the formation of the New Model provided enough men for the entire regiments of Fairfax and Whalley, with a cadre left over to form a basis for other units.

Once the New Model cavalry became organized the regimental strength settled down at six troops of 100 men each.

The colonel and the sergeant-major each commanded a troop, the remaining four being led by captains. Troop officers were a lieutenant, a cornet and a quarter-master. The colonel's troop was frequently led by the senior lieutenant of the regiment since, as in the infantry, the colonel was often a general officer, absent on other duties.

The cavalry are one instance in the New Model of strengths being up to establishment, and sometimes even over the required figure. In the force Cromwell led to Ireland in July 1649 he had an overstrength regiment of horse of 14 troops under his personal command. This was subsequently split in two, and Cromwell's major, Thomas Shellbourne, was given command of the second regiment.

**The Artillery**

There was no set organization for the artillery, but for major field actions the New Model usually had a strong artillery train. Initially of 56 pieces of various calibres, the artillery doubtless grew in size as captured equipment was absorbed. Two companies of what were termed 'firelocks' accompanied the artillery. These were infantry armed with flintlock muskets, whose rôle was the protection of the gunners, the artillery train, the powder store and the wagon park generally. The issue of the latest type of hand-held firearm to these troops was essentially a safety measure. Their duty required them to be in constant proximity to the artillery train where, more than anywhere else in the army, there tended to be loose powder exposed in open barrels, or split in the heat of an action. The presence of musketeers with ever-burning slowmatches would have been unacceptably hazardous; the chronicles of the Civil Wars offer us many examples of tragic accidents of this type. Major Desborough was the officer in command of the 'firelocks' at the formation of the New Model, and his men seem to have numbered around 120 or 130.

A company of pioneers was attached to the main artillery train; these worthies seem to have enjoyed semi-civilian status—certainly no uniform details are recorded. Their function seems to have been to assist in the passage of the artillery train along what passed for roads in 17th century England.

**The Staff**

The 17th century English army had a surprisingly large and organized staff. Serving directly under the commander-in-chief (in the New Model in 1645, Sir Thomas Fairfax, the Lord General of Parliament's forces) was the Lieutenant-General of the Horse—a post initially filled in the New Model by Oliver Cromwell (1599–1658). This

officer ranked as second-in-command of the entire army and commander of all the cavalry of that army. Below him was the Commissary-General of the Horse, the second-in-command of the cavalry. Below the Commissary-General were two Adjutant-Generals of Horse; a Quarter-Master-General of Horse; and a Muster-Master-General of Horse (this officer, at the outset one William Stone, had two deputies, and was responsible to the Treasury for the army rolls). The cavalry staff was completed by a Markmaster-General of Horse and a Commissary-General of Provisions.

The Sergeant-Major-General of the Foot had command of all the infantry in the army, and was the third-ranking officer in the overall hierarchy. To assist him he had a Quarter-Master-General of Foot and an Adjutant-General of Foot. The fourth-ranking officer in the army was the Lieutenant-General of the Ordnance, who controlled the artillery and engineers. Attached to the headquarters establishment was a Judge Advocate, with two Provost-Marshal-Generals, one of foot and the other of horse. A Commissary-General of Victuals was responsible for the difficult task of keeping the army fed while on campaign.

★　★　★

Between 1645 and 1660 a number of new regiments were raised. In all the New Model had some 28 regiments of horse, 62 of foot, and four of dragoons; not all these were in existence simultaneously, but the majority were. From the small beginnings of 1645 grew an army which, although naturally of variable fighting quality, generally proved to be of impressive battlefield value, and which laid down the organizational and tactical blueprint for the

Restoration army of King Charles II, and thus for the generations of British soldiers who came after them.

# Uniforms and Equipment

With the formation of the New Model Army a degree of uniformity began to appear at army level for the first time. While the cavalry retained the trusted and proven 'buff coat', the infantry were clad in coats of a uniform Venice red colour. This said, it must be emphasized that throughout the Civil Wars any true uniformity that existed was at a strictly regimental level, coats of similar colour appearing in both Royalist and Parliamentarian armies. Contemporary accounts often tell of officers galloping up to lead a unit into action only to find that 'their' men were in fact the enemy; there were numerous examples of luckless officers being taken prisoner in this way, and others of quick-thinking gentlemen escaping in the confusion by tearing off the 'field signs' which were usually all that distinguished friend from foe.

The troops' clothing was supplied by Parliament, who purchased materials and equipment as and when it was needed. Several contractors were employed, serving the needs of the various regiments as directed by Parliament.

A misconception which is still current to some extent is the idea that the army of Parliament was soberly dressed, and that its soldiers had close-cropped hair, while the Royalists were richly dressed and affected flowing locks. This was not at all the case. The fallacy seems to have taken root from a few accounts of the very early days of the war, when passions were running high and factions were very marked within the various forces. Some Puritan groups—by no means a majority of Parliament's forces—are believed to

**A matchlock musket and rest, c.1600—this was still the main source of infantry firepower in the early years of the New Model, although flintlocks gradually replaced it. (NAM)**

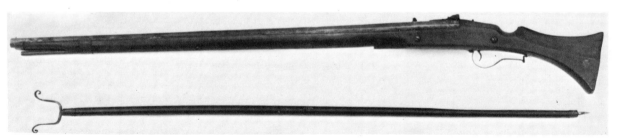

have worn their hair cropped, simply as part of their everyday style of life, and at that early and chaotic stage such extremes of appearance would be remarked upon. Generally it is true to say that the Civil Wars split English society 'vertically', not 'horizontally'; the men of great aristocratic dynasties and the sons of labourers were to be found in both armies; while the full range of costume styles observed in the community would be found in the ranks of both. This fact is underlined by the constant mentions of the importance of 'field signs'—sashes or scarves of different colours, ribbons, even scraps of paper or bunches of leaves—adopted by the two armies during the various campaigns.

## The Infantry

The infantry helmet was falling into disuse during the First Civil War due to its weight and general awkwardness; its use generally prevailed, however, and it is fairly certain that the pikemen of the New Model, at least, were issued with metal helmets. The general style was that of a morion, a basin-shaped skull with a wide brim and a reinforced central spine or comb. It was tied or buckled under the chin by thongs or straps, the upper parts of which were fitted with steel plates to protect the sides of the face. There were variations, but this basic style was the norm.

The wide-brimmed felt hat was more popular with the musketeers, and gradually came into favour with pikemen as well. With a fairly high crown, and often decorated (apparently at the

**Breast plate, helmet and back plate preserved at Broughton Castle, and probably worn by one of Lord Saye and Sele's men. The corselet is unremarkable; note that the joining straps at shoulder and waist are missing. The helmet is more interesting; it has much broader, shallower lines than the usual 'lobster-tail pot', and two very large cheek-guards, which presumably buckled tightly closed on each side of the face, producing a helmet with an overall appearance similar to a burgonet. What type of soldier wore this helmet we cannot be certain, but it is probable that he was mounted. This is a reminder that while the classic 'pot' may have represented the norm, a wide variety of helmets of many nationalities and ages was worn during the Civil Wars.**

owner's whim) with a feather or plume, the 'slouch' hat was a simple, utilitarian item of everyday outdoor wear, which became practically universal by the time of the Restoration.

The Monmouth cap, possibly named after its actual or supposed place of origin, was also worn, but its precise appearance is uncertain; certainly it was knitted, and could have a tassel, so we may assume either a skull-cap, or something resembling a stocking or fisherman's cap, sometimes with a falling end.

The coat or 'cassock' was the largest single piece of 'new' equipment provided for the New Model. This was a combination of jacket and overcoat, a long-sleeved, button-through garment which reached initially to the hip-bone but later became much longer than any of its Civil War predecessors. When Cromwell was equipping the expedition to Ireland in 1649 he ordered '15,000 cassocks of venice red colour, shrunk in water with a like number of breeches of grey or other good colour'.

It is difficult to find pre-Restoration pictorial evidence of the cassock, but there is ample from

'Musketeers or fusiliers and cavalry, about 1650'—a much later and rather unconvincing reconstruction, but interesting in that it accurately depicts the full impedimenta carried by a matchlock musketeer: between the two central figures we can make out the 'Twelve Apostles', bullet bags, a large powder flask and a small priming flask, and lengths of spare match. The rider is taken from engravings of 'harquebusiers', probably from Cruso's *Militarie Instructions for the Cavall'rie* of 1632. By the 1640s the 'harquebus' had generally disappeared among English cavalry, though the long saddle-pistols were still carried; and this old name for a cavalryman was still in use. The helmet seems to resemble in some respects the Broughton Castle example. (NAM)

the period after 1660. Since it seems unlikely that the Restoration army was dressed in any very radically different fashion from the successful army of the Commonwealth and Protectorate, it is suggested that the cassock evolved in the ranks of the New Model. The inadequacies of the makeshift equipment of the early Civil War armies would have been shown up under campaign conditions in the period 1642–45; and it may be suggested that the cassock was a solution to the need for troops in the field to have the protection of some kind of overcoat.

While the army would have tailors in its employ, and would avail itself of local civilian skills, it seems unlikely that all Cromwell's 15,000 cassocks could have been altered to give each soldier an exact fit. Since the cassock was intended as a protective garment it is not unreasonable to assume that it had some kind of lining. It also seems safe to assume that a musketeer given a coat or cassock (the terms seem to have been interchangeable by the time of the Restoration) which 'nearly' fitted him would turn back the sleeves at the cuff in order to load, prime and fire his musket conveniently. In doing so he would naturally expose any lining. In the opinion of the writer, this may well have been the beginning of the use of sleeve turnbacks as coloured regimental distinctions. It is, at least, as logical a theory as any other to explain the vexed question of the coloured linings listed, but tantalizingly unexplained, in some contemporary records of regimental clothing which pre-date the formation of the New Model—

e.g. Edward Montagu's regiment in 'red lined white', and the Earl of Manchester's in 'green lined red'.

Shirts and doublets were still worn under the cassock, but would only be visible if the latter was worn unbuttoned. Trousers or breeches, as noted above, would have been of a drab colour, grey being mentioned by name. The most popular style was a loose, baggy cut gathered just below the knee and tied with a band. Two pairs of stockings or hose could be worn, an outer woollen pair over a cotton inner pair, at the choice of the individual. There seems to have been little or no attempt at uniformity; simple unbleached materials of light drab shades seem logical. The shoes of the day were low-sided, tied or buckled at the front over a tongue, and of brown or natural leather. Each man was usually issued with two pairs.

## The Cavalry

The cavalry helmet was the reliable *zischagge*, or 'lobster-tail pot'. Basically this had a round skull with attached front peak, neck-guard and ear-guards. Neck-guards were often of true or simulated 'lames', that is, narrow horizontal strips rivetted along the edges—thus the 'lobster-tail'. Some styles featured a face-guard of one or three bars dropping vertically from the peak, while others had none. There was no standard pattern, and since English-made and imported Continental helmets were both used in great numbers it is pointless to seek one.

The coat of 'buff'—'buffalo' leather by old tradition, but in fact of cow hide—was the basic garment of the cavalryman throughout the Civil Wars and afterwards, being worn with or without the additional protection of a metal back-and-breast cuirass. Buff coats were expensive—roughly the same price as a horse—so Parliament was doubtless glad to be relieved of the burden of such an expense when forming the New Model horse: for most troopers would certainly have possessed them already. The use of armour in the cavalry, as in the infantry, was on the decline; it is likely that the cumbersome metal back-and-breasts would have disappeared gradually during the period under consideration, although the helmet was retained.

There is little or no evidence that the cavalry adopted any red uniform items in parallel with infantry practice, but here we are forced into pure speculation. Some buff coats had long sleeves, often with double upper sleeves; others did not protect the arm, or had long sleeves buttoning up their whole length which were often worn open and thrown back from the shoulder, exposing the doublet. Contemporary engravings show, in some cases, what are clearly decorated sleeves, with braid in vertical and horizontal bands. This suggests that the sleeves are those of a cloth doublet exposed by a sleeveless buff coat; and these sleeves were undoubtedly coloured. The degree to which the Venice red of the New Model foot was used must remain a mystery.

Trousers, of sober colour and hard-wearing materials, would often be of a tighter fit than the baggy infantry style, since they had to be worn tucked into the riding boots—which were perhaps the trooper's most important garment after the buff coat. They were of thigh length, and when pulled fully up for riding gave considerable protection. The toes were generally square, in the fashion of the day, and the heels fairly high; massive spurs were normal, with large 'butterfly' guard-leathers at the instep. The 'bucket' tops of the boots could be folded down when dismounted, and are often shown worn in this way in contemporary pictures. Special over-stockings called 'boot hose' were normally worn under the boots to protect the finer hose worn next to the skin. Two thousand pairs of boots described as 'of good neats-leather, well tanned and waxed' were purchased for the Irish expedition.

## The Dragoons

Although there were instances of them charging as a formed body of horse, as at Naseby, it seems probable that it was the exception rather than the rule for them to wear the back-and-breast. Such armour would have little value in their normal round of duty, and would hamper them in the handling of the firearms which were their normal weapons. Both the wide-brimmed slouch hat and the 'lobster-tail pot' were probably observed, depending on weather and duty. The infantry coat or cassock was worn by the dragoons of the New Model; since it was a button-through item it presented no problems for a rider. In the early stages of the New Model's career there are references to 'tawny' coats: we may speculate that Venice red might have become the norm later on. It seems perfectly likely that a fair number of buff coats would also have been observed. Trousers and boots probably resembled cavalry style since the amount of time spent actually fighting dismounted was short compared with the hours spent in the saddle.

★ ★ ★

The officers of the New Model Army were probably a law unto themselves in the matter of dress. They were drawn from every section of society, from the wealthiest aristocrats to the yeoman farmers and the urban mercantile middle class: Cromwell's beloved 'plain buff-coated captains'. Costume would reflect wealth and background, and contemporary civilian fashion—there was no separate tradition of military clothing at that period. The amount of lace and braid, feather plumes, and rich embroidery which an officer

**Surviving Continental example of the musketeer's bandolier of charge-containers and canvas bullet bag. The perils and inconveniences of using this equipment are discussed in the text. (G. A. Embleton)**

affected was dependent on his pocket and life-style. Cloaks could be short and fashionable, or long, enveloping and practical. The suits of full or three-quarter armour in which successful or wealthy officers had their portraits painted were almost unknown on the battlefield during the New Model period.

## Weapons

### The Pike

The pike, 'an honourable weapon' in the estimation of Major Elton in his *Compleat Body of the Art Military* of 1650, was the standard weapon of the infantry from its introduction in the 15th century until its disappearance in the early 18th century. Officially 18ft long, although more typically of 15–16ft, the stave was of well-seasoned ash. The slim steel head was socketed to the end, with long metal strips projecting between two and four feet down the sides of the shaft and rivetted to it, to prevent opportunist cavalrymen from lopping off the business end of the weapon. Since this unwieldy weapon's value rested solely on its use *en masse*, to provide a defensive hedge of points or to force formed bodies of enemy foot from the field 'at push of pike', there was a complex drill comprising many postures designed to give bodies

of pikemen the maximum flexibility of response and dexterity, despite the built-in disadvantages of their weapon. (That these were recognized at the time, despite the continued use of the weapon for another 70 years, is confirmed by such commentaries as Lupton's *Warre-like Treatise of the Pike*, published in 1642.)

### The Sword

The normal sidearm of a 17th century gentleman was the slim, rapier-style sword, carried by officers of both horse and foot entirely at personal whim; styles of hilt and degrees of decoration were subject only to individual taste. The rank and file carried no standard pattern of sword, in any arm of the service, before the Restoration. General Monck called for all pikemen and musketeers to be armed with 'a good stiff tuck', in other words a thrusting rather than a cutting weapon. Any swords made for mass-issue to the infantry would be cheaply made and of simple design, and doubtless of very variable quality as well. The cavalry were issued with various types of basket-hilted broadsword. The yard-long blades were double edged and could deliver both a cut and a thrust. It was chiefly this class of weapon that was supposedly nicknamed 'mortuary sword' due to the hilts of some examples being worked into the resemblance of the head of King Charles I. (This is one of those neat stories which has made a long career for itself, but whose actual contemporary provenance is suspect.)

### The Musket

The most common firearm in the armies of the day, and the principal weapon of the infantry in the period under consideration, was the matchlock musket. This tended to be a fairly standardized weapon, with a 48in. barrel firing bullets of just over an ounce weight. Accurate only up to about 50 yards, the musket was militarily useful only when employed by massed formations; but the heavy, low-velocity ball inflicted massive splintering wounds on any soldier unfortunate enough to be hit. The drill for its use was slow and complicated. Gunpowder was poured down the barrel from a flask, or from one of a number of containers each holding a pre-measured charge. The ball was dropped into the barrel, and rammed home with a wad of cloth to hold it in place. The priming pan

**Musketeer's powder flask of *c*.1650, typical of the equipment of New Model infantrymen. (NAM)**

at the breech of the musket was then filled with a finer-grain powder from another flask, and covered until the moment of firing with a swivelling lid. The weapon was too heavy to allow a steady aim from the shoulder without a support, and the use of a fork-topped rest under the barrel was universal during the early years of the Civil Wars. (It seems likely that a reduction in the weight of muskets, and the adoption of new mechanisms allowing less robust construction, led the use of rests to be abandoned gradually during the latter years of the New Model.) The match, a length of cord impregnated with saltpetre or vinegar, was held in front of the priming pan in the jaws of a serpentine arm, with its end smouldering. At the moment of firing the pan cover was swivelled aside and the trigger pulled, the simple internal mechanism of the lock thus dropping the burning end of match into the priming powder. The ignition sent a spark through the touchhole to the main charge and fired the musket after an appreciable pause, producing choking clouds of smoke which on windless days soon hung thickly over both armies and obscured their view.

In windy or rainy weather—hardly unusual in England—the musketeers' reliability was drastically curtailed; and under all conditions the necessity of keeping lengths of match glowing

**Farndon Church windows depicting two Royalist officers. Despite the deterioration many details of contemporary costume may be made out; see Plates A, C, F, and G.**

throughout an engagement, and of avoiding accidents due to the presence of hundreds of naked flames and much loose powder, further limited the tactical flexibility of such troops. The mixed formation of pikes and muskets, which went some way towards balancing the weak points of one weapon with the advantages of the other, was a direct consequence of the weapons technology of the day.

The paraphenalia necessary for the use of the matchlock musket was considerable. Slung over one shoulder the musketeer usually wore a broad leather belt from which were suspended on cords a number of small wood, tin or leather bottle-shaped containers for pre-measured powder charges— traditionally there were twelve, popularly known as 'The Twelve Apostles', but numbers varied. A bag of bullets was usually attached to this belt as well. From this or another sling hung a small flask of priming powder; again, a simple cut-off device in the nozzle often dispensed a measured amount. A larger flask or horn contained coarse powder for replenishing the charge containers, or for immediate use, as time and circumstances allowed. Lengths of slow-match would be carried at some convenient point on the clothing or equipment— in wet weather, often stowed under the hat. With the musket, the rest, a sword and often a 'snapsack' for rations, the musketeer was miserably encumbered.

As already mentioned, the more modern flint-lock musket or 'firelock', whose self-contained firing mechanism did away with the need for smouldering match, was carried by some troops. These included the artillery guards, and also mounted troops such as dragoons and some of the cavalry—the complexities of matchlock weapons obviously made them unsuitable for riders. The degree to which flintlock carbines were carried by regiments of horse is uncertain, but was probably dependent on economic factors. Flintlocks were more expensive, requiring special manufacturing skills which were less widely available, and a higher degree of maintenance and skilled repair facilities. Nevertheless their obviously important tactical advantages led to a steady increase in their use by the New Model during its lifetime, and by the time of the Restoration a high proportion of the infantry carried flintlocks.

## The Pistol

Apart from their broadswords, troopers of horse also carried a pair of 'horse pistols' in saddle holsters. There were many different models of these sturdy but inaccurate weapons, whose use was limited to close-quarter fighting. Both flintlock and wheel-lock designs were used. The latter type were fired by a spark produced by the release of a 'clockwork' mechanism, a coiled spring enclosed in the lock and tensioned by engaging a 'spanner' over an external lug. They were efficient weapons by 17th century standards, but were obviously much more complex, and thus more expensive and harder to maintain in the field, than other types of firearm. All types of pistol were of fairly massive construction, being between 18 and 24in. long.

★ ★ ★

All the general types of weapon described above were extensively used during the life of the New Model Army. In addition there was widespread use of personally owned weapons, not only swords passed down by previous generations of a family, but also hunting guns and fowling pieces, particularly among officers. Weapons of Continental origin were also in widespread use.

## Artillery

The New Model was generally well-supplied with artillery. The guns came under two main categories: those for siege work, and those for field actions. In the siege train were the 'cannon' of varying calibres, firing balls of between 30 and 60lb. Such guns played a vital part in the siege of Edinburgh Castle during Cromwell's invasion of Scotland, and were similarly employed during the Irish campaign.

The field guns rejoiced in a large number of different names, and to add to the confusion some pieces had more than one title. The heaviest piece likely to be seen in the field was the culverin, which could fire a ball of 16 to 20lb over a maximum range of some 2,000 yards, although something of the order of 800 yards was more typical. The demi-culverin fired a 9 to 12lb projectile to about half the range of the culverin, while the saker, probably the most commonly used field piece, had a ball weighing 5 to 6lb. Many other light pieces were interspersed between these main types, as there was no set system of pattern, calibre or poundage among the artillery.

Field guns generally had an immediate crew of three: the gunner, who supervised and positioned the gun; the gunner's mate, who loaded; and a helper. (Much larger groups were needed for man-handling the guns, of course.) Guns could fire at a rate of approximately 10 to 15 rounds an hour, depending upon the calibre of both gun and crew. Wherever possible the artillery was deployed in batteries, and if the situation permitted the positions were protected by gabions—earth-filled baskets. Gun carriages were painted grey—'a fair ledd colour'.

Powder was carried in barrels and ladled into the guns. Normally the projectiles were solid spherical shot of stone, lead or iron, but shells—spherical iron cases full of powder, with short lengths of fuze—were beginning to appear. These tested the skill of the gunner to the full, as the fuzes had to be cut to exactly the correct length to produce the desired delay.

The artillery train of the 17th century army moved very slowly, and made enormous demands on both man- and horse-power. The average field piece needed between six and eight horses or oxen in the draught team; given that the New Model artillery train in 1647 numbered 56 pieces, plus siege equipment, and given the large numbers of wagons needed to transport associated supplies, an idea of the numbers involved can be gained.

**Illustration from a tract of 1648, 'The Humble Petition of Jock of Bread', which shows in quite recognizable cartoon form the contemporary form of gentlemen's dress; note officer on right, with halberd, sash, and large turned-down boots. (G. A. Embleton)**

## Flags

The system of flags adopted during the Civil War was continued after the formation of the New Model.

The infantry had one colour per company, i.e. ten in all. The colonel's flag was completely plain, being dyed in whatever colour the regiment had adopted, usually at the choice of the colonel; e.g. when Charles Fairfax, uncle of Sir Thomas, was given command of a Yorkshire regiment of foot in 1648 he adopted for their flags his family colours of blue and white. The lieutenant-colonel's flag was similar, with the addition of a St George's Cross on a white canton in the left upper corner. The sergeant-major's flag was the same, with the addition of a 'pile wavy'—a 'flame' shape projecting diagonally down and right across the field from the bottom right corner of the St George's Cross canton. The captains' flags employed a device—e.g. a five-point star, mullet, cross, lozenge, etc.—in a contrasting colour to the field of the flag. The flag of the first captain's company would be similar to that of the lieutenant-colonel, but with one example of this device added in the middle of the field. That of the second captain would carry two devices, that of the third captain three, and so forth up to seven. An occasional variation was the use of a 'first captain's' flag by the sergeant-major, in which case the first captain's flag bore two devices, and the seventh captain's eight. Some colonels opted for variations on their personal arms, however. These generally observed practices were not governed by any rigid regulation. The flags themselves were usually made of taffeta, with the design painted on the cloth. The field of the infantry colour was usually 6ft 6in. square.

The cavalry carried standards at troop level, so there would thus be six in most New Model regiments of horse. They were usually about 2 foot square, and did not follow the infantry pattern of markings; complete, simplified, or extracted versions of the regimental colonel's flag were normal. Political cartoons, a hangover from the early days of the Civil War, were not unknown—though much of the point or 'humour' is inevitably lost on modern readers.

Dragoon regiments had a system based on infantry practice, but with cavalry-sized standards or guidons of swallow-tail shape. They carried varying numbers of the regimental device to indicate company numbers.

The main commanders of the army each had personal standards, and these may or may not have been used in the field to mark the positions of headquarters.

# Army Life

## Recruiting

Despite Parliament's stated aim in forming the New Model, it should not be presumed that it was in fact a willing, able body of soldiery ready to 'go anywhere and do anything'. Originally the planned strength was 14,400 infantry, but this proved hard to achieve in reality. Waller's old command provided 600, Essex's army 3,000, and Manchester's 3,500. To fill out the ranks impressment was employed—not a method conducive to attracting recruits of prime military quality or unshakeable loyalty. London and the south-east were the main hunting grounds for the 8,500 men required. This quota was followed by another of 4,000, which meant that in real terms a majority of the New Model infantry were 'pressed men', liable to desert whenever opportunity arose. In spite of the activities of the press gangs, the New Model was still 4,000 under strength at the beginning of the Naseby campaign in spring 1645. A further impressment took place in 1651 in order to raise the 10,000 men needed for the Irish campaign.

After some initial unrest in 1645 the army settled down, and an amazingly low number of desertions is recorded—although the impartiality of these records is naturally open to question, since the uses of propaganda were well understood in the 17th century. It would seem, however, that apart from the immediate periods of the 1645 and 1651 impressments the ranks of the New Model were largely filled by volunteer recruits. A proportion of these were 'turned' ex-Royalist prisoners, who may be presumed to have been of dubious fighting value.

A very basic and erratic local regimental affinity system also began to emerge, with some regiments recruiting only in specific areas, such as Montagu's Regiment of Foot, which was composed of men from Cambridgeshire.

While impressment was necessary to fill the ranks of the infantry, the cavalry rarely had such problems, despite the fact that a recruit had to provide his own mount and, on occasion, his own equipment. The gentry of the day would always opt for the cavalry, and the rural population provided large numbers of experienced riders. Instances of cavalry regiments over-subscribed by twice the required numbers are mentioned elsewhere in this book.

## Pay

The subject of pay—or rather, arrears in pay—was a constant bone of contention among the men of the New Model.

The rates of pay did not remain constant between 1645 and 1660. On the formation of the army in 1645 an infantryman received 8d (in modern terms, 3p) per day, a cavalry trooper 2s (10p), and a dragoon 1s 6d ($7\frac{1}{2}$p). In 1649 the price of wheat had soared to double that of 1645—inflation is not a 20th century invention—and pay was accordingly adjusted. An infantryman was paid 10d (4p) per day in the field or 9d ($3\frac{1}{2}$p) if in garrison; a trooper 2s 3d (11p), and a dragoon 1s 9d ($8\frac{1}{2}$p). The period 1651 to 1655 saw the infantry in Scotland receiving much the same level of pay,

while a trooper had an extra 3d, making 2s 6d ($12\frac{1}{2}$p) a day, and a dragoon drew 2s (10p).

In 1655 the cost of living evidently fell, for pay was reduced to a level which was maintained until the disbandment of the New Model in 1660. Infantrymen drew 9d ($3\frac{1}{2}$p) in the field and 8d (3p) in garrison; cavalrymen 2s 3d (11p), and dragoons 1s 8d (8p).

The payment of infantry officers had remained constant; presumably they were thought to be above the effects of inflation, since the concept of an officer living on his pay would have been unknown in the 17th century. A colonel drew £1 per day, a lieutenant-colonel 15s (75p), a sergeant-major 13s (65p), a captain 8s (40p), a lieutenant 4s (20p), and an ensign 3s (15p). Senior cavalry ranks also drew a constant rate throughout the period: 22s (£1.10p) for colonels, 15s 8d (78p) for sergeant-majors and 10s (50p) for captains. There were three main changes in the pay of junior cavalry ranks, however. In 1648 a lieutenant drew 5s 4d ($26\frac{1}{2}$p), in 1655 7s 6d ($37\frac{1}{2}$p), and in 1660 6s (30p). Cornets had similarly dated changes from 4s 8d (23p), to 5s 4d ($26\frac{1}{2}$p) and 5s (25p). The

A showcase of surviving Civil War equipment and clothing in the National Army Museum, London. The sleeveless buff coat is displayed with a large gorget; on the right is a trooper's typical three-bar 'pot', a corselet displaying the armourer's proof mark, and a bridle gauntlet. The latter was usually worn only on the left arm, to protect in battle the rein hand. (NAM)

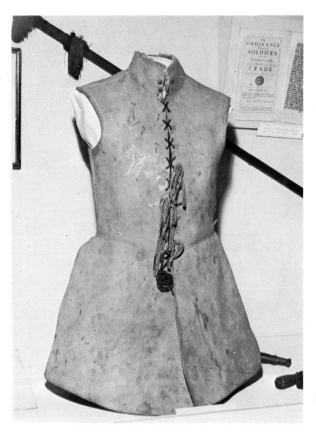

Close-up of the buff coat in the previous picture; probably the most popular item of dress among soldiers of both armies, it was expensive but highly prized for its combination of lightness, convenience, and good protection—it could turn a sword-cut. Many different styles were worn, with or without stand collars and sleeves, with buttons or laces, and sometimes with quite costly decoration such as thin leather sleeves with bullion lacing. It could be worn under a cuirass or without additional protection. (NAM)

horses, the number of which varied with rank. In 1651 a colonel could claim for six horses at 2s per day each, thus adding 12s (60p) to his basic pay of 22s (£1.10). Other officers could claim for their horses on a *pro rata* basis. This system seems to have been more strictly limited in peacetime, and by the Restoration the colonel could claim for only three mounts.

It should not be presumed that the rates of pay quoted here all went into the soldier's pocket. Approximately half the pay of a private or trooper, and about one-third of an officer's pay, was deducted to pay for clothing and 'free quarters'. There were also deductions for food when the army was on the march. The nett result was that the enlisted man saw precious little of his few pence a day.

Generals and senior officers were subsequently given additional rewards in the shape of grants of land. In 1645 Cromwell himself was granted lands by Parliament worth £2,500 annually; his success at Worcester in 1651 brought a further £4,000 in property grants. Personal gifts were not uncommon either; after Naseby Fairfax was given 'a fair jewel set with rich diamonds of very great value' ('jewel' in those days meaning a piece of jewellery-work, probably a type of pendant). The fortunate few who captured enemy colours could also expect financial reward, whatever their rank. Such worthies each received 10s (50p) after the battle of Dunbar.

Plundering was officially frowned upon but, as throughout history, it was in fact up to the individual general in the field to apply or ignore the theoretical regulations. Some commanders offered their men extra pay to prevent the plundering of a captured town or castle; others 'looked the other way' for 48 hours or so.

## Supplies

Due to the lack of an organized army commissariat, soldiers were generally quartered in civilian homes, the unfortunate owner being obliged to provide food and accommodation for a stipulated number. The expense was re-imbursed to the householder at a fixed rate, endorsed by a ticket given to him by a commissariat officer which bore details of numbers housed, for what period and so forth. In sad fact Parliament did not fall over

regimental quarter-master drew 4s (20p) per day throughout the period.

Contemporary sources also provide us with a useful comparison in the form of the pay rates for certain staff officers. Captain Sykes, Provost-Marshal-General of Foot in the New Model, received 4s 5d (22p) per day, and his 20 men 2s (10p) each. The Advocate of the army received 10s (50p), and his clerk 3s 4d (16½p). This clerk apparently drew the same daily rate as the Provost-Marshal-General of Horse; and the regimental provost-marshals of both horse and foot also drew 3s 4d daily. The Army Scoutmaster-General received a handsome £4 per day, but out of this had to pay two or more 'spies' and a troop of 20 men.

Cavalry officers had an additional source of income in that they could claim extra monies for themselves to honour these tickets when they were presented for payment, and remunerations were frequently and continually deferred. This method of billeting was understandably unpopular, although Parliament did issue strict rules designed to ensure fair treatment for soldier and householder alike. Apart from quartering its men on the civilian population the New Model frequently requisitioned supplies from the surrounding area, these requisitions being once again backed by a promise of payment—eventually . . .

As time passed and the New Model became better organized, both of these systems gradually ceased to be employed, to the relief of the civilians. By 1651 Cromwell's commissariat department seems to have been able to cope with the army's needs, although many supplies arrived in the form of 'voluntary' contributions from the people of the vicinity. However well-organized the supply system may have become by 17th century standards, it was still rudimentary at best, with the army constantly short of food. Once abroad in Scotland and Ireland the problem of hunger became acute; and a case can be made out that it was Cromwell's forced delay in Dublin while awaiting supplies which allowed the Irish rebellion to gain strength. Contemporary sources underline the constant complaints from commanders in Ireland about the food shortage.

On campaign the average soldier's rations consisted of bread and cheese. Biscuits were often substituted for bread, and the odd 'liberated' fowl or animal would doubtless provide some variety; but bread and cheese was the staple diet on which the soldier of the New Model marched and fought. The official daily ration per man was one pound of bread and half a pound of cheese, the former usually carried on the soldier's person, the latter on pack-horses.

Possession of castles or other strongpoints meant that supply dumps could be built up to feed an army on the march, and the route of a marching army was often dictated by the location of these sites. Some sutlers' wagons often accompanied the march; they could sell goods to the troops at fixed prices set by the army's Provost-Marshal-General. Overall, the commissariat of the New Model coped better than most 17th century establishments, and made definite improvements upon the early Civil War systems with which they had started.

## Discipline

Despite the proclamation of disciplinary codes by several commanders—Leslie, Essex, and Ormond among others—the newly formed New Model inherited much of the ill-discipline of the early Civil War armies from which it was raised. Looting, poaching and outright theft were all accepted as a way of life by the rank and file.

Fairfax and Cromwell used their authority to support the disciplinary codes, and had several officers to assist them in this context. The chief legal officer of the army was the Judge Advocate, who was responsible for drawing up charges and supervising the observance of legal niceties at trials. His staff are listed earlier in this book. These

**A Farndon window depicting a drummer of the period.**

officers had the responsibility for the custody of prisoners, and the carrying out of punishments after verdict and sentence. Each of the two Provost-Marshal-Generals had some 20 men under direct command as what we would term military policemen. Another task of the PMGs was to set the prices of the goods sold by the sutlers, and to ensure that they gave good measure. In addition, as mentioned earlier, each regiment had its own Provost-Marshal, so there was a reasonable number of officers and men available to enforce everyday discipline.

Punishments, predictably enough, varied with the severity of the crime. Mutineers were either hanged or shot; plunderers were whipped, and more minor misdemeanours earned the luckless culprit a session astride the wooden horse, a sharp-angled trestle frame. Blasphemers ran the risk of having their tongues bored through with a red-hot iron. Punishments were sometimes coupled together: a lashing of a typical 30 strokes would be followed by the victim being forced to 'run the gauntlet' between the ranks of his comrades, or to endure the 'strappado'—being jerked agonisingly into the air by his bound wrists. Once the initial resentments natural enough among pressed men had been overcome, the army gradually became a reasonably well-disciplined body. The popular image of the God-fearing, law-abiding Puritan soldier can have had only limited validity among the ranks of the New Model as a whole, but there were vast improvements over the behaviour of their early Civil War predecessors. One can imagine that the average soldier was much more afraid of his Regimental Provost-Marshal than he was of his God.

The large-scale mutinies which disturbed the New Model at specific periods, due to the volatile political situation, naturally fall outside this brief summary of everyday disciplinary problems. Revolutionary armies throughout history have been prone to incidents such as these; and in the New Model, as throughout history, they were swiftly and ruthlessly crushed by loyal troops.

## Religion

The largest religious group within the New Model were the Independents, coming from the armies of Waller, Essex and Manchester. The popularity of this belief spread, and by the end of 1647 it was virtually universal in the army. Presbyterian officers either left the army, or were removed from any posts of influence. There was a constant interplay of religious opinions and dogmas throughout the army, but the triumph of the Independent faction also had a political dimension. When army and Parliament fell out an overwhelming proportion of the officers—Independents—supported Cromwell and Fairfax; the Presbyterians sided with Parliament, and were promptly replaced for their pains.

There seem to have been only a handful of chaplains with the New Model, and initially there were none at regimental level—another fact at variance with popular belief. The few that there were made up for their lack of numbers by an almost frenzied activity. The office of Chaplain to the Army was not held by any one man for any length of time. It was the Chaplain's duty to deliver heartening sermons on the eve of battle and, in the event of victory, to organize thanksgiving services of prayers and psalms.

There were only five ministers with the army between 1645 and 1646, all of them Independents, naturally enough. When Cromwell moved into Ireland he took with him two chaplains, neither of whom stayed long. The invasion of Scotland in 1650 presents a very different picture, however. Each regiment apparently had its own chaplain; but it would seem that this was less from concern with the spiritual well-being of the army than with the hope that the Scots could be persuaded to embrace Independent principles by sheer weight of clerical numbers following the more martial 'softening up' process.

Six chaplains went with General Venables to the West Indies in 1654, but only one remained by 1657. In Flanders the army seems to have been totally devoid of ministers. It would appear that the initial enthusiasm of the majority of would-be chaplains waned under the rigours of campaigning. It was apparently fairly easy to fill the relatively 'glamorous' post of Chaplain to the Army, but far less easy to persuade clerics to operate at a humbler regimental level.

The policy of Parliament on this issue is unclear, but it seems that they made no strenuous efforts to maintain any set number of ministers with the

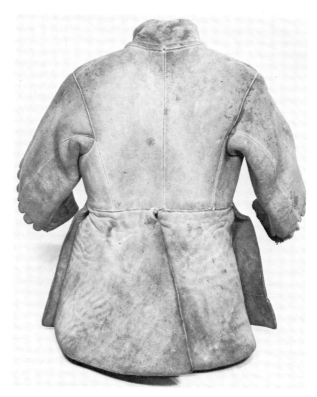

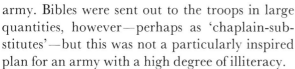

Details of a fine example of the ubiquitous buff coat, apparently worn by a cavalryman—Major Saunders of Gell's Horse. The overlapped skirts keep the coat closed over the abdomen and groin when the wearer is mounted; the heavy over-sleeves on the upper arms give added protection to an area often vulnerable to sword-cuts, while the cut-outs at the elbow allow free movement. Note the thickness of the hide, visible at the scalloped edge of the over-sleeve; and woven leather buttons at the rear of the cuffs and on the collar. (NAM)

army. Bibles were sent out to the troops in large quantities, however—perhaps as 'chaplain-substitutes'—but this was not a particularly inspired plan for an army with a high degree of illiteracy.

Another popular idea is that the men of Cromwell's New Model were fond of singing psalms, and this does seem to be supported by contemporary accounts. Several officers also took it upon themselves to preach their own ideals to their comrades; doubtless this helped to fan the flame of Independency, certainly in 1647–48 when the idea had a certain novelty value. The concept of soldiers preaching to their comrades caused uneasy questions to be asked in the House, and by the summer of 1653 statutes were introduced in an attempt to regulate what went on. (One is forced to conclude that this unease sprang from a concern for orthodoxy and discipline, rather than from a human pity for tired men harangued in their camps when they would rather have been enjoying their meagre comforts!) The gradual outcome was that a type of Congregationalism emerged as the main religious feeling, and the character and mood of the army were modified as a result.

## Marriage

Initially there was no official opposition to soldiers of the New Model marrying, and many did. Records show wives and sweethearts travelling with the army on the march and moving freely about the camps. The trouble started when the army began to serve abroad in Scotland, Ireland and the West Indies. After a campaign the army returned to a base camp, and the marriage rate generally accelerated at a smart pace. The men of the New Model frequently took local wives, and this began to concern the generals. They reasoned that their men might suffer weakened allegiance, or might give away military secrets. On 1 May 1651 Cromwell issued a proclamation banning marriages in the army. Offenders were cashiered, although cavalry troopers could transfer to the infantry instead.

It is interesting to note that logically the proportion of volunteers in the army must have been high by 1651 for dismissal on marriage to have been a real threat. It would have been a simple way home for mere pressed men.

## Medals

After the victory over the Scots at Dunbar in 1650 medals were awarded to the common soldier for the first time. An artist was sent to Edinburgh to sketch Cromwell's likeness so that it could be engraved on the medal. Cromwell resisted this idea, and offered alternative designs; these were rejected, however, and the Dunbar medal carried his image. It appears that gold medals went to generals and other high-ranking officers, silver medals to more junior officers, and, possibly, copper medals to the rank and file—although it is not confirmed that the common soldiers did in fact receive their medals.

# Campaigns

The first major test of strength for the New Model was to come at Naseby. The summer of 1645 found the king with a capable, veteran field army whose main fault was lack of numbers—three years of war had taken their toll of the Royalist ranks. After the successful Royalist storming of Leicester the king's army faced the New Model near the village of Naseby in Northamptonshire (14 June 1645). The king's troops came close to victory, but eventually Cromwell's well-trained cavalry decided the day, and the main Royalist field army was destroyed.

After Naseby, Lord Goring had the only Royalist army capable of doing battle with the New Model, and he was engaged in besieging Taunton in the West Country. Fairfax at once moved to the relief of the town, forcing Goring to abandon the siege and to adopt a defensive posture near Langport, Somerset. Fairfax's 10,000 men defeated Goring's 7,000, and proceeded to mop-up the remaining Royalists in the area before turning on the keystone of Royalist power in the west—Bristol, held for his uncle by no less a commander than Prince Rupert himself. The importance of this port was increased by the fall of Royal strongholds elsewhere, including Pontefract and Scarborough Castles. Fairfax encircled the city, and took some of the outer defences; Rupert's subsequent surrender on terms was a shattering blow to the Royalist cause. After some minor skirmishes the last Royalist army in the field was defeated at Stow-on-the-Wold on 21 March 1646. The First Civil War was over; and the New Model had gained valuable experience in two major field engagements, a siege, and a number of smaller affrays.

## The Interim

After the cessation of active hostilities King Charles continued to negotiate for support with anyone who would treat with him; in desperation he surrendered to the Scots, who subsequently handed him over to the English. Confined under conditions of relative freedom, he continued to intrigue for allies who might help him regain his throne.

Since the work of the New Model appeared to be done, and since they lacked funds to honour arrears of pay, Parliament wished to demobilize the Army. The troops objected, predictably, and there was a period of some turmoil. Under cover of these factional arguments the king escaped from captivity at Hampton Court and reached Carisbrooke Castle on the Isle of Wight. The Army blamed Cromwell for this, and it took his presence in person to avert a major mutiny; despite his success, the habit of indiscipline lingered on below the surface.

## The Second Civil War

In 1647 King Charles signed 'The Engagement': a treaty with the Scots by which he undertook to set up the Presbyterian Church in England if they supported his bid for restoration. The Scots invaded England, and Royalist embers inside the country were fanned into new flame; the main concentrations were in Essex, Kent, the northern counties and South Wales. Fairfax dealt with

1. Musketeer, Earl of Manchester's Rgt., pre–1645
2. Infantry officer, Thomas Ballard's Rgt., pre–1645
3. Pikeman, Lord Saye and Sele's Rgt., pre–1645

A

1. Officer of pikemen, c.1645–50
2. Soldier in siege armour
3, 4. Pikemen, c.1645–50

B

1. Officer of musketeers, Lord Fairfax's Rgt., *c.*1645–50
2, 3. Musketeers, *c.*1645–50

C

1.  Dragoon, *c.*1645–50
2, 3.  Troopers of Popham's Horse

D

Gun crew, c.1645–50

1. Senior cavalry officer, *c.*1645
2. Sir Thomas Fairfax, *c.*1645
3. Major John Desborough, *c.*1645

F

1. General George Monck, 1650's
2. Oliver Cromwell, 1650's
3. Senior officer, 1650's

G

See Plates commentary for standard details

1

2

3

4

5

6

7

DIVINIS
PRO
QVI ADMITTIT SERVM
HVMANIS
VIM VI

FIDELITER·
·FAELICITER·

ORA ET PVGNA IVVET
ET IVVARET IEHOVA

PRO
PACE
PVGNO

BEATORVM
BELLA        BELLA

H

Essex and Kent while Cromwell moved to re-capture Pembroke from the rebels. It is worth examining in some detail the dispositions of the New Model at this stage, i.e. April/May 1648.

Colonel Horton had been sent to South Wales to supervise the disbandment of Laughane's Royalist regiment; he had with him Butler's Regiment of Horse (which he now commanded); three troops of Fleetwood's Horse; eight companies of Okey's Dragoons; and Lloyd's Foot. The total was some 900 horse, 1,000 foot and 800 dragoons. When Cromwell moved to assist Horton he brought with him Sheffield's Horse and the infantry of Hammond, Harley and Pickering.

Hardress Waller was active in the West Country, and had with him his own regiment of foot supported by the two remaining companies of Okey's Dragoons and Pye's Horse. Gloucester, strategically important since it covered the crossings of the River Severn and thus communications with South Wales, was garrisoned by Montagu's Foot. Five companies of Ingoldsby's Foot held Oxford, always a trigger-spot for Royalist risings. Thornborough's newly raised regiment of cavalry was dispersed to patrol North Wales.

Newcastle was held as a Parliamentarian stronghold in the North, by Sir Arthur Hesilrige with his own regiment of foot and that of Skippon (under command of Lt. Col. Ashfield). The able Major-General Lambert, soon to figure prominently in events, had in the North a strong army of three cavalry regiments (Rossiter's, Hesilrige's and his own) and a regiment of foot under Col. Bright, with two more infantry regiments forming. Lambert was soon reinforced by the Lord General's (Fairfax's) Foot, two troops of Fairfax's Horse, and the whole of Sheffield's regiment.

The rest of Fairfax's Horse stayed in London with Fleetwood's, Whalley's, and part of Rich's. Fairfax's Foot were also in the capital initially, with the other five companies of Ingoldsby's and the whole of Pickering's and Tichbourne's (the latter a newly raised regiment based on the Tower of London).

As the military picture developed, so Fairfax was forced to spread the New Model extremely thinly to guard against all eventualities, the mounted troops in particular being moved about from one trouble-spot to the next.

After dealing with some other outbreaks, Fairfax moved on Kent and Essex. With Rich's Horse and Fortescue's Foot he occupied Southwark, mustering the remainder of his force at Hounslow. The rebels fell back before him as he advanced via Blackheath, Eltham, Gravesend, Meopham and Malling. The nominal commander of the Royalists in Kent was the Earl of Norwich, father of Lord Goring; he was determined to oppose any crossing of the Medway. He had some 4,000 good troops and a less impressive gathering of 7,000 ill-armed rebels. These he deployed in and around the town of Maidstone.

Fairfax avoided attempting a defended river crossing, marching to cross the Medway at Farleigh Bridge and turning back to attack Maidstone. After bitter fighting he forced the Royalists out of the town (1 June 1648). Ireton, with his own cavalry regiment and Fortescue's Foot, ably supported by Col. Rich leading Pye's Horse and Pickering's Foot, succeeded in subduing the rest of the area.

June saw Fairfax recrossing the Thames at Tilbury to deal with the rebels in Essex. He moved from Billericay towards Colchester with some 5,000 men: Whalley's, Fleetwood's and Ireton's Horse, his five companies of Ingoldsby's Foot, and the whole of Tichbourne's ('The Tower') Regiment of Foot. He came up against a meagre Royalist force led by Sir Charles Lucas, who held the Prince of Wales's commission as general of the Essex Royalists. Three Parliamentarian assaults were repulsed, until weight of numbers forced Lucas to withdraw into Colchester town (11 June). Fairfax besieged Colchester, which capitulated on 28 August.

*The Battle of Preston, 17/18 August 1648*
While Fairfax was occupied in the south, Cromwell had to deal with the Scots invasion. Murmurings by pro-Royalists in Scotland culminated in the assembly of an army under the Duke of Hamilton. Though a useful figurehead, and well-connected in England, the Duke was not of the calibre of, say, Montrose. Matters came to a head with the seizing of Berwick by Sir Marmaduke Langdale, and shortly thereafter both Pontefract and Scarborough Castles declared for the king. Hearing of the Pembroke rising, Hamilton set out

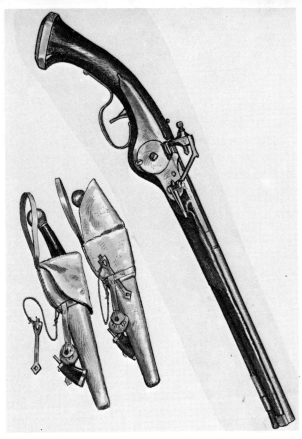

A simple military wheel-lock pistol of the 17th century, typical of issue to New Model troopers. The detail shows the use of one type of saddle-holster, with flask, bullet bag and pistol-spanner attached. (G. A. Embleton)

Scots at Walton after fording the river.

An incident now occurred which is typical of the confusion of war. The Scottish cavalry, led by Middleton, had come up from Wigan to assist their comrades at Preston, but did not arrive until after dark. Missing the Royalist infantry, they stumbled upon Cromwell's men, who had by now reached Walton in their pursuit of Langdale and Hamilton. Middleton turned and fell back, pursued by Thornhaugh's Horse; but shortly afterwards hunter became prey, when Middleton turned again and counter-attacked, routing the New Model troopers and killing their colonel.

During the confused night of retreat and pursuit Langdale's cavalry escaped northwards, and was eventually disbanded. Most of his infantry surrendered. The Scottish infantry were rounded up and captured after a brave stand at Winwich, 20 miles south of Preston. Another 2,600 Scots were captured at Warrington. Langdale escaped to the Continent, but Hamilton was finally caught at Uttoxeter.

Cromwell's forces at Preston were as follows: *Horse* Rossiter's, Thornhaugh's, Sheffield's, and his own. *Foot* Fairfax's, Lloyd's, Rainsborough's, Harley's, and two Lancashire regiments under Col. Ashton.

Arranging terms with the shattered Scots without difficulty, Cromwell moved on to take Pontefract, the Royalist bastion in Yorkshire. His victory there marked the end of the Second Civil War.

## The Regicides

Seemingly undismayed by the failure of his Scots allies, the king still took a confident tone in his negotiations with Parliament. The army commanders were determined that Charles should not again escape the consequences of his intrigues, which they classed as treason, and the New Model was soon at odds with Parliament. The soldiers demanded sweeping constitutional changes; the Presbyterian MPs were equally determined to rid themselves of the army and to come to some sort of agreement with the king. Events came to a head on 6 December 1648, when Col. Pride marched down to the House with a body of musketeers and prevented 100 Presbyterian members from taking their seats. (King Charles's example had borne

in that direction with an army of 10,000, crossing the border early in July and linking up with Langdale's 3,000 foot and 600 horse. A further small reinforcement came from Ireland, under Sir George Munro. Unfortunately for Hamilton, Cromwell speedily subdued Pembroke; he then marched to support Lambert, who had been entrusted with operations in the North.

By 16 August Cromwell was at Stonyhurst Park near Preston, having marched via Pontefract, Leeds and Skipton. His army was small—some 8,500 men—but of fine quality. The Royalists were moving south from Carlisle via Lancaster when Langdale discovered Cromwell's whereabouts. Langdale held the bridge over the Ribble at Preston in a gallant attempt to buy time for the Scottish infantry to cross and reach Wigan, where the Royalist cavalry were stationed. Hamilton had to come to his rescue, however, and both were finally surrounded. The Scots crossed safely, and Langdale and Hamilton managed to extricate a large part of their force and to join the bitter fruit.) In effect this reduced the Commons to a 'Rump' of approximately 50 members.

Cromwell was adamant that further dealings with Charles were pointless. On his urging, the Rump Parliament passed an ordinance on 6 January 1649 establishing a court to try the king. When the House of Lords refused to endorse this radically unorthodox step it was abolished. The trial was a constitutional mockery; whatever his faults, Charles did not lack courage and dignity, and his bearing before this tribunal was impressive. The trial ended on 27 January 1649, with the only verdict possible. On Tuesday 30 January 1649 Charles Stuart died, like a king and a gentleman, on the block in Whitehall. (It is pleasant to record that Sir Thomas Fairfax took no part in the trial or death of the king, as a matter of principle.)

## Ireland

Catholic and Protestant Irish alike were united in their condemnation of the Regicides; such was the height of feeling that by midsummer 1649 only Londonderry and Dublin remained loyal to Parliament. After consultation with Fairfax,

Cromwell was appointed to lead an expedition of 12,000 men to deal with the uprising: four regiments of horse, four of foot, and some companies of dragoons. The selected troops were offered the unenviable alternatives of service in Ireland, or disbandment. The mutinous feelings caused by this insensitive order were only soothed by the intervention of Fairfax himself.

The first to sail were Cromwell's double-strength regiment of horse; that of Lord Broghill, of similar size; the conventional cavalry regiments of Graves and Hacker; and the foot regiments of Hammond, Pickering, Rainsborough and Cromwell. Okey's regiment provided the dragoons. Subsequently cavalry regiments led by Henry Cromwell, Michael Jones, his brother Theophilus Jones, Edmund Ludlow (soon to be Lieutenant-General of Horse in Ireland), John Ponsonby, John Reynolds and Sir Charles Coote all arrived

This is thought to be an interesting example of an elderly but serviceable helmet up-dated for use at the time of the Civil Wars: the skull is that of an Italian barbutte-style helmet of the 15th century, but the peak is much later and resembles that of a conventional 17th century 'pot'. (Department of the Environment (Crown Copyright)

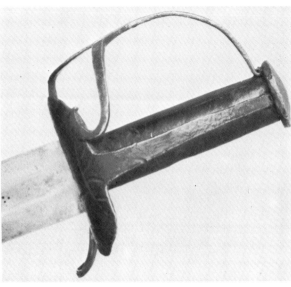

Hilt detail of a 'mortuary sword'; a cartouche with the crowned head of King Charles I can be made out worked into the guard. (Below) A much plainer type of hilt, typical of the Civil War trooper's weapon of what might be termed 'ammunition quality'. (Department of the Environment/Crown Copyright)

all crossed with Cromwell, and the colonels tended to move from one regiment to another, but all the named regiments saw service in Ireland during the campaigning there. Most had been raised before or during the Second Civil War, and several were raised after the Irish campaign had begun.)

After an artillery bombardment of Drogheda which lasted two days, Cromwell launched a general assault on 10 September 1649. It was repulsed, as was a second attempt. A third assault, reputedly led by Cromwell in person, was successful. It was followed by a grisly massacre of the captured garrison and the civil population alike, which Cromwell justified on the grounds of military expediency and—quite openly—of religious hatred for the Catholics. This atrocity, which has continued to haunt Anglo-Irish relations down the centuries, had its desired effect in that it cowed some other rebel strongholds into surrender; but in as many cases it steeled resistance, and the garrison and citizens of Wexford were subjected to a comparable massacre when they, too, were finally overcome.

Although the New Year of 1650 saw the army ravaged by dysentery, spotted fever and malaria, which killed more men than fell in battle in this campaign, Cromwell went on to capture Kilkenny and Clonmel after costly fighting. His return to England in May was attended by a hero's welcome. Although the Irish did not finally admit defeat until 1652, the back of the rebellion had been broken and only small and dispersed rebel forces remained.

## Dunbar and Worcester

Taking advantage of Cromwell's preoccupation with Ireland, the Scots proclaimed the late king's eldest son as Charles II and invited him to Scotland from exile. Fairfax, long troubled by the direction political events had taken, and by the use which had been made of his name by extremists, used his recent inheritance of a Scottish peerage as his reason to refuse command in the campaign against the Scots, and retired from public life. His post of Captain-General passed to Oliver Cromwell; Lambert became Major-General and second-in-command, with General Fleetwood as nominal commander of the cavalry and General Monck

in Ireland. The new dragoon regiments of Abbott (ex-major in Okey's) and Ingoldsby (a short-lived unit) soon sailed to add their weight to the expedition; as did infantry regiments commanded by Axtell, Barbase, Castle, Clarke, Cole, Fenwick, Gifford, Huncks, Hungerford, Ingoldsby, Ireton, Kynaston, Long, Moore, O'Connolly, Phayne, Reeves, Saunders, Stubber, Tothill and Venables. (It must be emphasized that, as was the case with New Model regiments of earlier raising, not all these regiments were active simultaneously; not as commander of the Foot.

On Charles II's arrival in Scotland in summer 1650, the Marquis of Argyll organized a new Scots army for him; field command was given to General David Leslie, the Covenanter soldier who had fought alongside Cromwell at Marston Moor in the First Civil War. In July Cromwell crossed the border from Berwick with some 11,000 foot and 5,000 horse, the cream of the New Model. Leslie conducted a skilful campaign, falling back across 'scorched earth' to strong positions before Edinburgh. Cromwell's army, suffering from want and disease, was forced to retreat in its turn on its supply port of Dunbar. Leslie followed, and got astride Cromwell's line of retreat to England. On 3 September 1650 Cromwell launched a daring dawn attack. His first wave was repulsed; indeed, a unit of lancers among Leslie's cavalry even drove back some of the veteran New Model horse. A fierce two-hour infantry mêlée followed, at the end of which Leslie's right began to fold under pressure, exposing his centre. Cromwell committed his cavalry reserves in a brilliantly timed attack, routing the Scots right and centre. Nevertheless Leslie succeeded in leading much of his cavalry and his left wing of foot back to Stirling in safety.

Cromwell's forces at Dunbar were as follows:
*Horse* The Lifeguard of Fairfax, Fleetwood's, Rich's, Vermuyden's, Lambert's (ex-Northern Counties Assoc.), Lilburne's, Hacker's (new unit, raised late 1648), and one other veteran regiment.
*Foot* The Lord General's, Harley's, Lloyd's, Monck's (part of Lloyd's, part of Weldon's), Charles Fairfax's (West Riding of Yorks.), Malevere's and Bright's (both ex-Poyntz's army), Daniel's (diverted from Irish army), and one other, known to be partly from Guernsey, partly from Hull. In addition there were two companies of dragoons from Okey's

Edinburgh Castle surrendered to Cromwell's men on Christmas Eve 1650 after a hard siege; but his troubles were far from over. On New Year's

Day 1651 Charles II was formally crowned by the Scots at Scone. During the first half of 1651 Leslie manoeuvred with skill, avoiding pitched battle. Cromwell, handicapped by recurring bouts of malaria, was receiving reinforcements, but they were raw troops. The young king and his hot-blooded supporters overruled the cautious Leslie and ordered an invasion of England when Cromwell's manoeuvres took him out of the Covenanters' path.

The Royalist army marched by way of Carlisle to Worcester, where they halted to rest in the hope of reinforcements from Wales. Cromwell was held up at Perth, but sent General Lambert and his cavalry ahead to harry the Scots and delay their progress. This he did with partial success; but it was only when Cromwell himself arrived with the rest of the army, after moving via Doncaster, Coventry and Evesham, that Charles's route to London was fully barred. Charles ordered Worcester fortified, and the bridges across the Severn destroyed. Combing the area for boats, Cromwell constructed a floating bridge which he left under the care of Fleetwood; in the meantime Lambert's troopers had been scouting with a will, and found a usable bridge still intact. On 3 September 1651, one year to the day after Dunbar, Cromwell attacked over both the permanent and the floating bridges; according to tradition he led the latter attack himself. At one point his army was split by the Severn, but the Royalist attempt to exploit this situation failed. When the Scots tried to break out eastwards Cromwell recrossed the river and personally led the decisive counter-charge. The Royalists were totally defeated after a last stand in the city near the town hall. Charles II eventually escaped to the Continent, and long exile. Worcester, Cromwell's 'crowning mercy', is generally regarded as his finest victory, which

**Cavalry broadsword, c.1640, typical of the better type of Civil War trooper's weapon. The iron basket hilt is of the type known as a 'mortuary sword'; the blade is about 36in. long. (NAM)**

Fine example of a mid-17th century cavalryman's flintlock carbine; note 'dog-lock' and ring for belt-catch, and deeply carved butt. (Department of the Environment/Crown Copyright)

finally brought to an end the Civil Wars.

It is not certain which regiments actually fought at Worcester on 3 September, but all the following are known to have taken part in the Worcester campaign: *Horse* Fairfax's, Hacker's, Lambert's, Pye's, Rich's, Rossiter's, Sheffield's, Vermuyden's, Whalley's, plus one other. *Foot* Bright's, Charles Fairfax's, Ingoldsby's, the Lifeguard, Harley's, Malevere's, West's.

## The Commonwealth

With the end of the fighting the political tensions once again came to the fore. The army still wanted Parliament dissolved, while the Commons called for the demobilization of the army. Feelings ran high; and in 1653 army officers submitted a scheme for a new system of government.

Cromwell, supported by Major-General Harrison and a company of musketeers, brought the confrontation to an abrupt close by expelling the 'Rump' of the Long Parliament from the House. He appointed a Council of State, which nominated the short-lived 'Barebones Parliament', but this in its turn was dissolved in December 1653. Lambert and a council of officers drew up the 'Instrument of Government', giving executive authority to a Lord Protector and the Council of State. On 16 December 1653 Oliver Cromwell, ex-captain of cavalry from Huntingdonshire, became Lord Protector of England, Scotland and Ireland.

The country seethed with unrest as both Royalists and factions such as the Levellers plotted to overthrow the regime. Cromwell's spies penetrated the Royalist secret society, the Sealed Knot, and kept him advised of its plans. In the event the only rising which took place came in March 1655, led by one Colonel Penruddock; it was put down by Major-General Desborough at South Malton in Devon. To increase his hold on the country Cromwell divided it into military districts, each governed by one of his major-generals with local militia and cavalry units (see map).

### Jamaica

Spain was at war with England, and Cromwell despatched Admiral Blake to protect English shipping from the harassment of Spanish warships in the Mediterranean. Many successful actions were fought; Blake, and Cromwell's other 'Generals-at-Sea', laid the foundations for Britain's later naval supremacy.

In December 1654 Admiral Penn and General Venables set sail for the West Indies with a vague brief to attack Spanish interests in the area. Venables had five weak regiments of poor-quality infantry—2,500 in all—raised specifically for overseas service: Venables's, Hearne's, Buller's, Carter's and Humphrey's. Each was strengthened to 1,000 men, mainly by recruiting among indentured servants at Barbados, and a sixth, Doyley's, was raised. Local recruiting and subsequent reinforcement from home added four more regiments: Moore's, Holdep's, Fortescue's (ex-colonel of foot in the original New Model), and Brayne's Horse. Holdep's was raised in St Christopher and the Leeward Islands during February–March 1655.

In April 1655 the expedition landed on the

island of Hispaniola, but was repulsed by Spanish forces, Venables's own regiment suffering particularly heavy casualties. No second attack was mounted; on 5 May the army sailed for Jamaica, where it landed unopposed five days later. On returning to England, claiming ill-health, both Penn and Venables were imprisoned for returning without orders. Fortescue was left in nominal command. The regiments remained in the West Indies until paid off and disbanded after the Restoration.

## The Battle of the Dunes, 14 June 1658

In October 1655 Cromwell had signed a treaty of alliance with France. In 1657 some 6,000 soldiers of the New Model landed at Boulogne to add their numbers to the French army of Marshal Turenne, who was fighting the Spanish. Mardyk was taken, and in 1658 the Spanish sent a relief force to raise Turenne's siege of their stronghold at Dunkirk. Among the 14,000 Spanish troops were 2,000 exiled English Royalists, and the right wing of the Spanish army was led by James, Duke of York, younger brother of King Charles II. The New Model contingent in Turenne's army was commanded now by Sir William Lockhart (replacing the original commander, Sir John Reynolds); it consisted of Lockhart's own regiment of horse, and the foot regiments of Alsop, Clarke, Cochrane, Lillington, Morgan and Reynolds. The infantry were a mixture of veterans and new recruits. At the Dunes on 14 June the wily Turenne planned his conduct of the battle on the beach around the timing of the tide-change. The English foot fought on the left of his line, and were particularly praised for their steadiness in defence and spirit in attack. The Anglo-French victory cost only about 400 casualties, mainly among the New Model units, compared to some 6,000 Spanish. When Dunkirk fell it was given to England as her share of the spoils of victory.

## Towards Restoration

Oliver Cromwell, the victim of recurring illness, died on 3 September 1658. His elder son Richard, chosen by his father as successor, summoned his first Parliament in January 1659. He was unable to dominate the factions in the army and the House, however, and resigned from his empty title

in May. Considerable unrest followed, with various groups and officers manoeuvring for power. Sickened by the spectacle, and correctly judging the mood of the country, Major-General of Foot George Monck moved south from Scotland with his troops. He gathered much support from many quarters, and was named by Parliament as commander-in-chief with wide powers. He supervised the election of a new Parliament, which in May 1660 voted for the restoration of the monarchy. On 25 May 1660 Monck, the architect of the restoration, welcomed Charles II ashore at Dover.

Charles disbanded the army shortly after his return; England had had enough of martial law, and only two horse and two foot regiments were retained. These were to become the Grenadier Guards, the Coldstream Guards, the Life Guards and the Royal Horse Guards.

The New Model Army was no more.

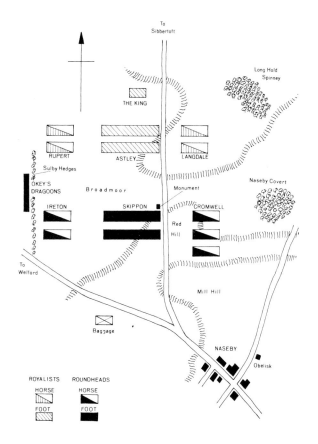

BATTLE of NASEBY 1645

**(Christopher Warner)**

# The Plates

Additional research by Chris Warner, using mainly the sources listed in the bibliography.

*A1: Musketeer, Earl of Manchester's Regiment, pre-1645*

This man's only protective armour is a 'secrete', a metal skull cap worn beneath the felt hat. His green clothing, with red lining, identifies his regi-

**England divided into Major-Generalships by Cromwell in 1655:** (1) John Lambert—Yorkshire and the North. (2) Charles Worsley—Lancashire, Cheshire and Staffordshire. (3) Edward Whalley—Lincolnshire, Leicestershire, Derbyshire, Nottinghamshire and Warwickshire. (4) James Berry—Worcestershire, Herefordshire, Shropshire, Monmouthshire and Wales. (5) William Boteler—Bedfordshire, Huntingdonshire, Rutland and Northamptonshire. (6) Charles Fleetwood—Oxfordshire, Buckinghamshire, Hertfordshire, Essex, Norfolk and Suffolk. (7) Philip Skippon with John Barkstead—London and Middlesex. (8) John Desborough—the West Country. (9) William Goffe—Sussex, Hampshire and Berkshire. (10) Thomas Kelsey—Kent and Surrey. (Christopher Warner)

ment; the white scarf round his hat was the field sign at Marston Moor, where this regiment fought with distinction. Some kind of field sign or 'field word' was generally used to distinguish friend from foe at this period, when clothing was often common to both sides. At Edgehill Essex's army wore tawny-orange scarves; at Newbury, 'green boughs', in their hats (i.e. a bunch of green leaves). At Marston Moor those who had no white cloth wore scraps of paper. In a minor skirmish at Bangor both sides independently decided to wear no field signs, with doubtless confusing results. As mentioned in the text, the removal of the sign in the nick of time often allowed men to avoid capture or death; Fairfax narrowly avoided capture at Marston Moor by removing the paper from his hat, passing unharmed through the Royalist ranks. At Edgehill Sir Faithfull Fortescue's troop of horse deserted to the King, but several were killed by the Royalists before they could tear off their scarves.

His armament consists of a matchlock musket, supported in action on the rest seen here slung from the shoulder; and a broadsword carried on a baldric. Neither the standard barrel length (48in.) nor the standard bore were strictly adhered to, producing a quartermaster's nightmare. Describing the use of muskets of different sizes by the English army in Ireland, Lord Orrery recommended '. . . that all our muskets be of one bore, or at most of two sorts of certain bore, the bigger for the stronger, the smaller for the lesser bodies; for want of this I have seen much hazard undergone.' He speaks of musket balls being generally too large for the weapons carried, '. . . whereby we had like to have been worsted; for the soldiers were forced to gnaw off much of the lead, others to cut their bullets; in which much time was lost, the bullets flew a less way and more uncertainly; and which was worse so many pauses animated the enemy by making him think our courages cooled.'

Sir James Turner describes the charge as being two-thirds ball-weight of 'common' powder, with half the ball-weight in 'fine' powder for priming the breech. The term 'bandolier' was variously applied, sometimes to the whole equipment of shoulder belt, measured charge holders of leather, wood or tin ('Twelve Apostles'), bullet bag, priming flask or tube, and often a large reserve flask of common powder, and sometimes to individual charge holders. The measured charge tubes are believed to have originated in the Low Countries. In action several bullets were often carried in the mouth, for speed. The bandoliers were inconvenient and sometimes dangerous. In high wind, or when running, a body of musketeers rattled so loudly that words of command were drowned, and of course destroyed any element of surprise. A stray spark could sometimes ignite the Apostles, with horrifying results. Lord Orrery: '. . . And when they take fire they commonly wound and often kill him who wears them, for likely if one bandolier takes fire, all the rest do in that collar . . .'

He goes on to mention an alternative method of carrying ammunition, which we cannot depict with any certainty, but which was obviously a kind of belly-box worn under the doublet and cassock: '. . . Whereas the cartridge boxes exempt those who use them from all these dangers and prejudices; they enable the soldiers to fire more expeditiously; they are also usually worn about the waste [sic] of the soldier, the skirts of whose doublet and his coate doubly defend them from all rain that doth not pierce both, and being worn close to his body the heat thereof keeps the powder dryer, and therefore more fit to be fired in service.'

In action the match was lighted at both ends and held in the left hand, being clamped into the cock only after priming was complete, and being removed after firing for the re-loading sequence. Inexperienced or agitated musketeers sometimes went out in a spectacular blaze of glory through absent-mindedly digging their flasks into the 'budge barrel' for more powder without removing the burning match from their fingers. A 'link' or coil of two or three yards of match was carried on the belt. The amount of match used was enormous, since it had to be kept alight throughout an action. The State Papers for 1644 mention that the garrison of Lyme, numbering 15,000 men, often used five hundredweight of match daily.

### A2: Infantry officer, Thomas Ballard's Regiment, pre-1645

He is dressed in a slightly outdated style more typical of the 1630s—but it should be remembered that much clothing and armour of earlier periods .

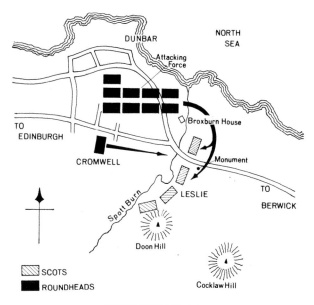

BATTLE of DUNBAR 1650

**(Christopher Warner)**

would still have been seen during the Civil War. The 'cloak-bag breeches' reaching to just above the knee were generally replaced by the 1640s by types reaching slightly below the knee. His 'cup-topped' boots are also rather old-fashioned, but have the fashionable red heels and soles. The spurs, with large 'butterfly' leathers, must have been awkward to wear when on foot, but they seem to have been common in Foot units. For protection a back-and-breast and a gorget are worn over a buff coat. The weapons are a partisan, traditionally the mark of officer rank for nearly two centuries, and a sword. The orange-tawny sash is traditionally associated with Parliamentary forces; however, while it was certainly worn as a field-sign from time to time, it is not really known how universally it was worn otherwise, or what exact colour it was.

### A3: Pikeman, Lord Saye and Sele's Regiment, pre-1645

The cap may have been known as a 'montero', from the Spanish for a mounted man, and normally associated with mounted troops. This widely-discussed cap, reinforced here with iron bands, would have been just as convenient for a foot soldier as a cavalryman. The rear flap could be worn up or down. Thomas Elwood the Quaker describes himself wearing on one occasion 'a large montero cap of black velvet, the skirt of which being turned up in folds, looked, it seems, somewhat above the then common garb of a Quaker'.

Our pikeman wears a corselet (back and breast plates) and tassets covering the thighs; but, as mentioned earlier, there was at this time a considerable reduction in the use of armour throughout most of Europe. Tassets had virtually disappeared, it seems, and even the back-and-breast was out of favour with many. Sir James Turner, writing in 1671, conforms to his usual reactionary line in opposing most developments in the warfare of his time. Despite his contention that a pikeman needed all his armour, for the sake of morale as much as protection, he is moved to write: '. . . When we see battalions of pikes, we see them everywhere naked, unless it be in the Netherlands.' (Turner was to make similar observations about the disuse of full cuirassier armour by cavalry, and the later abandonment of pikes themselves.)

In his book of 1650 the New Model veteran Richard Elton noted that '. . . our companies consisting of one hundred men, two parts being musketeers, and a third pikes.' The latter were often picked from the bigger men, as much more strength was needed. The ash staves were coloured with 'aquafortis'.

### B: Pikemen of the New Model, 1645

It seems that red was a predominant, though by no means universal colour for coats before the formation of the New Model. An extract from *A Brief Relation of the Siege of Newark* by Lt. Col. Bury, 1644, mentions the 'Norfolk Redcoats'. At the same time Montagu's Cambridgeshire and Isle of Ely Regiment was supplied with red coats faced white, according to Thomas Buckley's account in the Exchequer Papers, 27 March 1644. In 1645 the county of Essex was ordered to send its quota of recruits for the New Model 'commodiously provided, as hath formerly been practised, with 1000 red coats lined with blue'. The newspaper *Perfect Passages* of 7 May 1645 states that Fairfax's Regiment wore red faced with blue, and that '. . . the men are Redcoats all, the whole army only are distinguished by several facings of their coats.'

Contracts placed with the supplier Richard Downes were for cassocks '. . . of Suffolk, Coventry or Gloucestershire cloth, and to be made three-quarters and a nail long [$29\frac{1}{4}$in., i.e. hip length], faced with bayes or cotton with tapestrings according to a pattern delivered to the committee'. As mentioned earlier, the 1649 orders specify cassocks 'of Venice Colour Red'. The breeches were to be of Reading cloth 'of Grey or other good colour, in length three-quarters one-eighth [$31\frac{1}{2}$in.] well lined and trimmed'. The cloth of both garments was to be pre-shrunk in cold water. Stockings 'of good Welsh cloth' were supplied. Two qualities may be deduced from differences of price (perhaps over- and under-stockings, as the use of two pairs was common?) Low laced shoes, costing 2s 3d to 2s 6d in our period, were charged to the troops' pay at a rate considerably higher than wholesale price. In all, clothing stoppages totalled 9d per week, 39s per year. Col. Doyley complained on behalf of the unpaid soldiers in Jamaica 'that a private soldier can give four shillings for a pair of ammunition shoes, that never received so much these three years'. There was apparently no supply of headgear at this period,

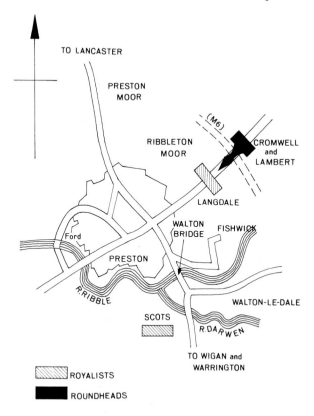

TO LANCASTER

PRESTON MOOR

RIBBLETON MOOR

(M6)

CROMWELL and LAMBERT

LANGDALE

WALTON BRIDGE

FISHWICK

Ford

PRESTON

R.RIBBLE

WALTON-LE-DALE

SCOTS

R.DARWEN

TO WIGAN and WARRINGTON

ROYALISTS

ROUNDHEADS

BATTLE of PRESTON 1648

(Christopher Warner)

34

and it may be assumed that each man brought his own.

### B1: Officer of pikemen

He carries, unusually, a 'pole hammer' in place of a partisan or 'leading staff' as his mark of rank. The doublet of Venice red is turned back at the cuffs to reveal the lining and shirt. A plain 'falling band' at the throat hangs down over the corselet and buff coat. He wears no boot-hose or spurs with his small bucket-topped boots; his overall appearance is plain, and his hair is cut shorter, in the manner of the Puritans—but see the reservations expressed in the body of the text about popular fallacies. His side-arm is a Flemish rapier of about 1625.

### B2: Soldier in siege armour

Note the very large helmet 'cage' and the metal shoulder-plates fixed to vertical bars at each side of the helmet; the rear guard was very plain and straight. This extra protection distributed the force of missiles which might be hurled from the walls, and the shoulder-plates helped support the weight of the helmet.

### B3, B4: Pikemen

Both wear the cassock, B4 with the blue lining of an Essex recruit; B3 has a falling band at the throat, B4 a knotted scarf. B3's helmet is a morion, B4's a cabacete, both common in this period. Heavy gauntlets were necessary to protect the hands from splinters and to give a better grip 'at push of pike'. B4 wears a 'Monmouth cap' taken from a surviving example in the Monmouth Museum—believed to be a genuine and unique survival from this period. The use of this type of cap lasted from the 16th into the 18th century, and was so common that no one felt any need to describe them. These woollen caps, made in quantity at Bewdley among other places, may have been intended for wear under a helmet, the back loop being for carrying and the button for securing (see Kirsty Buckland, 'Costume' No. 13, 1979). As early as 1544 an ordinance required '. . . every man to have a cap to be made to put his salette in.' In 1642 the Long Parliament provided the army in Ulster with 'Monmouth caps' at 23s per dozen. As helmets were discarded the cap was probably worn as an

Charles II—a later portrait after Lely. At the time of the Civil Wars, Charles was a courageous, if inexperienced young commander; his hairsbreadth escapes as he made his way to refuge on the Continent after the disaster of Worcester are legend—as witness the number of English inns called 'The Royal Oak'! On his Restoration in 1660 he inherited possibly the finest standing army in Europe; some units of the New Model saw action again, in Portugal, before the final dissolution which was politically inevitable. (NPG)

alternative; but the main replacement was a broad-brimmed felt hat. Tom Verney, who enlisted as a pikeman in Ingoldsby's Regiment in c.1653, requested provision of 'a grey Dutch felt'. Both B3 and B4 wear plain laced shoes over the usual coarse stockings.

On the ground are knapsacks or 'snapsacks'; New Model soldiers were issued these at 9d each, in which to carry food, clothing, and sometimes a tent portion. Paintings by Sebastian Vraux and Peter Snayers of Dutch troops in the Thirty Years War seem to show plain sacks with a belt at both ends, and this may have been the type used by the New Model, but since none have survived this is speculation. Water bottles were not issued—a major cause of disaster in the West Indies in 1655; with his men dying of thirst, Gen. Venables requested as essential a supply of 'leather bottles' or 'blackjacks'.

Monck's preference for a 'good stiff tuck' for the soldiers refers to a rapier or thrusting sword, as

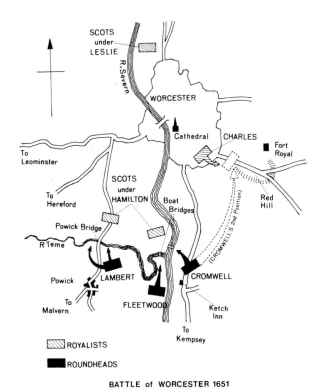

BATTLE of WORCESTER 1651

(**Christopher Warner**)

side-seams were also fully buttoned up their whole length. Beneath the cassock this officer wears a dark green doublet and breeches trimmed with silver lace. The richly embroidered gloves, with 'straps' on the inside opening, were common. Apart from his rapier this officer carries a 'leading staff', a lighter and flimsier version of the partisan, more practical as a mark of rank than as a weapon.

### C2, C3: Musketeers
Neither carries a rest, since the weapons were both lighter and shorter than formerly. C3 has a flint-lock weapon. The 'collar' or bandolier equipment on the ground is of a particular type which had a protective flap. Interestingly, the State Papers of April 1649 mention £100 paid for '1,000 collars of bandoleers, blue-painted in oil', and £75 paid for another thousand covered in black; but it is not known to whom these were issued. The other items of dress and equipment are discussed elsewhere; but note C3's surprisingly modern-looking wooden and leather clogs. Clogs are mentioned in use by some units in *Mercurius Brittanicus* of February 1646.

### D1: Dragoon
C. H. Firth considered that dragoons would probably have been equipped exactly like infantrymen, at least in the early years of this period. A. V. B. Norman of the Tower Armouries has considerable basis for believing that this was so; he has discovered that a musket sling of some kind was used, although the precise pattern is uncertain. (In Germany such slings were known a generation earlier, to judge by a print of a mounted matchlock-man published by von Wallhausen in 1616.) This dragoon wears smaller boots than a trooper—the boots were necessary protection in the saddle, but too full a top would make his movements as an infantryman very awkward. His weapon is a 'snaphaunce' musket, specifically recommended in Monck's *Observations* for these troops. Dragoon troopers carried no pistols, although officers presumably did; his only other weapon is a typical broadsword. The wide-brimmed hat was probably typical, and this countryman has added pheasant feathers. Later in our period a gradual move towards cavalry dress seems likely.

opposed to a cutting sword; he went on to say that '. . . if you arm your men with swords, half the swords you have in your army amongst your common men will upon the first march you make be broken with cutting of boughs.' This also suggests that issue swords were of less than brilliant quality. Sir James Turner thought hatchets would be a more practical issue, since cutting wood was about all that the swords were used for! Orrery says that in about 1660 few musketeers or pikemen carried swords at all. The sword of B4 is a hanger with a saw-backed blade, made in England in about 1630 and marked IOHAN KINNDT. That leaning against the pikes is one currently in the Tower Armouries.

### C1: Officer of musketeers, Lord Fairfax's Regiment
The only protective armour is a gorget, worn over a sleeveless buff coat of a type now held by the National Army Museum. The cassock, in Venice red lined blue for this regiment, is of the type which had the sleeves closed only by buttons up their whole length; these were often worn hanging loose, as illustrated. The front opening and the

## D2, D3: Troopers of Horse

Both wear the type of clothing and equipment known to have been issued to Popham's Troop of Parliamentary cavalry, several sets of which survive and are displayed at Littlecote House and at the Tower of London. Both wear variations of the 'lobster-tail pot'; D2 has a Continental-looking piece with fluting on the skull, lames on the cheek guards, and a single sliding nasal bar, while D3 has a more typically English style with a three-bar face guard mounted on an upward-swivelling peak, and plain surfaces. The lames of the neck-guard were often merely simulated with grooves. Heavy broadswords are worn from baldrics; note full or partial leather inserts in basket hilts. Both carry flintlock carbines attached by spring-clips to shoulder belts; these were usually unclipped for firing. A large flask for 'common' powder is slung on a cord. Presumably some provision for carrying balls and priming was made—perhaps these smaller items were slung to the holsters on the saddle for the wheel-lock or flintlock pistols?

Firth maintains that among regular cavalry, carbines were the exception rather than the rule, swords and pistols only being used, accounts for the New Model in the period 1645–46, and narratives of campaigns of that period both bear this out. However, between 1649 and 1660 carbines were much more generally issued.

It is not certain whether New Model troopers were issued the cassock along with the rest of the army. The buff coat was probably their everyday dress ('buff-coat' was the slang term for trooper at this time); but cassocks may have been worn when not on active service, certainly by officers. John Lilburne, a lieutenant-colonel of dragoons, is described as 'drawing a paper book from under his short red coat'. A lieutenant of horse quartered at Bristol attracted complaints by preaching publicly 'in his scarlet coat laced with silver lace'.

D2 wears his boots pulled up for riding, D3 has them folded down in the usual 'pedestrian' style. He also wears a single left-hand bridle gauntlet, to protect his rein-hand in battle.

## E: Gun crew

Artillerymen were not uniformed, and E1 to E3 are shown here in civilian costume. E1 is the gunner, E2 a helper, E3 the gunner's mate, and E4 a 'fire-lock-man'. The piece is a siege gun with a bore of 7in., firing a 40lb ball to approximately 1,700 yards. The gunner's mate loaded the piece, with the helper ensuring his supply of powder, ball, and tools. The gunner layed the gun, with the helper providing the muscle for the actual elevation and traversing; the gunner primed the touch-hole with fine-corned powder from his flask, keeping the vent clear with prickers carried in his satchel, along with other tools. He then fired it with the linstock. The soldier of Desborough's firelock companies—who appear to have been distinguished in the New Model by 'tawny' coats—carries a 'dog-lock' flintlock musket, with a safety catch hooking to the rear of the cock.

## F1: Senior cavalry officer

Two units are known to have fought for Parliament in full cuirassier armour: Sir Arthur Hesilrige's 'Lobsters', who were destroyed before the raising of the New Model, and Essex's Lifeguard. The use of this type of armour by individuals continued; and common sense suggests that it was limited to the wealthy and aristocratic, and perhaps to veterans of Continental wars who had acquired both the armour and the habit overseas. Portraitists continued to show such armour, but we may speculate that this was to maintain for their aristocratic sitters the traditional 'knightly' image. We show our senior officer in a German armour, taken from one currently on display in Zurich Museum, with a helmet of matching style. In battle, lamellar thigh defences would be added, worn with the usual high leather boots. A buff coat would be worn beneath the armour, which would otherwise provide little protection from impact. This officer has knotted the corners of his ornately laced 'falling band' together at the throat.

## F2: Sir Thomas Fairfax

'Black Tom', his left jawline disfigured by the huge, livid scar of the wound he received leading his cavalry into battle at Marston Moor, is shown here wearing only a gorget and buff coat as protection. The latter is of a style which featured thinner leather over-sleeves above the elbow. The embroidered crimson sash is conjectural, but by no means impossible. The use of crimson or 'rose'-coloured sashes is traditionally associated with

**Major-General John Desborough, originally commander of the two 'firelock' companies in the New Model, rose in rank and standing until in 1659 he overthrew the second Lord Protector, Cromwell's son Richard ('Tumbledown Dick'). His rising was put down in short order by the quick reaction of George Monck. (National Army Museum)**

Royalist officers, but as with Parliament's tawny sash, the actual conventions of use are unknown and were probably more liberal than we imagine. Sir Thomas Herbert speaks of Col. Harrison's meeting with Charles I en route to his trial, the colonel wearing 'a velvet montero on his head, a new buff coat upon his back, and a crimson silk scarf about his waist, richly fringed'.

### F3: Major John Desborough

We illustrate Desborough in a buff coat of a type with long sleeves of thinner, more supple leather added to the body of thick hide. The sleeves are closely hooped down their whole length with stripes of silver lace—a very common decorative style of the period, which has been misinterpreted from old engravings to justify showing Cromwell's troopers in something resembling Rugby football shirts! Vertical lacing, laced and buttoned sleeves, and combinations of these styles are all shown in portraits of the time. The coat's front is closed by

silver-lace clasps, and the boots have the fashionable red details.

### G1: General George Monck

George Monck (1608–70) was originally with the king's army in Ireland. Captured at Nantwich in 1644 and imprisoned in the Tower for two years, he joined the New Model on his release. As officer-commanding in Ulster he successfully carried out several small military expeditions. He went to Scotland with Cromwell in 1650, and was given overall command of the country. He remained there apart from a brief spell as a 'general at sea', and proved a popular overlord. It may be said that in early 1660 the fate of England depended solely upon this officer, who was centrally instrumental in bringing about the Restoration. He became Captain-General of the Army, Duke of Albemarle, Earl of Torrington and Baron Monck of Potheridge, Beauchamp and Tees. On his death he was given a state funeral paid for by Charles II, and was buried in Westminster Abbey.

He is shown in a fairly plain style suggested by a contemporary engraving. He wears his orange-tawny sash around the body rather than the waist, in a manner sometimes favoured by commanders. The dent in his breast-plate is the proofing-mark, the sign that the plate had resisted a test-fired pistol ball before being released. Note scalloped edge of the over-sleeves on his buff coat.

### G2: Oliver Cromwell

A Mazot portrait of Cromwell in the 1650s shows him in this costume of light brown velvet cassock and breeches, with a hat of matching colour decorated with three ostrich plumes, a plain collar over a gorget, and his boots pulled up for riding. He is unarmed. We felt this to be a slightly novel and more interesting subject than the half-armour or buff coat and corselet in which he is normally depicted.

### G3: Senior officer

This figure has been devised from features of contemporary portraits to show that Parliamentary officers could be just as ornately dressed as Royalists. The low, wide hat has a popular contemporary feature—a silver band. Rich lace appears at collar and boot-hose, and the baldric is richly embroidered. The rapier is taken from one now in the Tower Armouries. Note three-quarter over-sleeves on the buff coat, with thinner, buttoned cuffs of the under-sleeves visible at the wrist. The cords at the shoulders were known as 'arming points' and were a medieval survival used to lace on the vambraces of cuirassier armour. In the absence of armour they were often knotted up intricately to keep them conveniently out of the way, and they became accepted as one of the signs of a gentleman, and therefore an officer. In the next century they would become aiguilettes, specifically worn as a sign of rank.

## H: Colours and Standards

*H1* Believed to be a standard of Ireton's Regiment of Horse; approximately two feet square.

*H2* Colonel's colour, Charles Fairfax's Regiment of Foot—one of three raised in Yorkshire in 1648 to repel the anticipated Scots invasion. This West Riding unit served under Lambert and Cromwell, campaigned in Scotland, and was present at Worcester in 1651. The uncle of Thomas Fairfax, Charles chose his family colours for his standards. It is recorded that the flags were painted by 'Mr. Knight, a herault that dwells in Shoe Lane towards Fleet Street Conduit'. Approximately 6ft 6in. square.

*H3* Lieutenant-colonel's colour, Thomas Rainsborough's Regiment of Foot. In keeping with the Civil War pattern it is plain apart from the St George's cross canton. Approximately 6ft 6in. square.

*H4* Personal standard of Sir Thomas Fairfax. These personal standards would have been flown over command posts as a means of location, and may also have been carried by the general's personal escort. They were probably the same size as cavalry standards, but this may not invariably have been the case; we show this example enlarged for clarity of field detail.

*H5* Personal standard of Major-General Phillip Skippon. After a distinguished war record for Parliament Skippon became Sergeant-Major-General of Foot on the formation of the New Model in 1645.

*H6* Captain's colour, Twistleton's Regiment of Horse; typically, it bears a motto on a plain field, and would have been approximately two feet square. Philip Twistleton's regiment served under Lambert against the Scots in 1648 and after a brief posting to the North Midlands the next year spent most of its remaining life north of the border.

*H7* Captain's colour, Horton's Regiment of Horse. Colonel Thomas Horton took command of what had been Butler's regiment in June 1647. The regiment served with distinction in Wales, and then went to Ireland with Cromwell, where Colonel Horton died. The flag is fairly typical of

**An impression, by a much later hand, of an English musketeer of about 1670. The evolution of the costume of the New Model may be traced in this figure. The broad-brimmed hat, the many-buttoned coat and the cuffs with deep turn-backs exposing the lining all had their origins in the period 1645–60; these details are discussed in the text. (NAM)**

that of a cavalry captain; the arm and cloud were common throughout the regiment, with the motto and the device to the right changing from squadron to squadron.

---

## Notes sur les planches en couleur

**A1** Il n'y avait pas d'uniforme règlementaire, mais nous savons que cette unité portait des vêtements verts à doublure rouge. Une 'secrete' de fer sous le chapeau protège le combattant des coups d'épée. Il a avec lui un mousquet à mèche, èt des récipients en forme de bouteilles pour la poudre en bandouillière. Il a également une fourche pour reposer son arme pendant le tir. **A2** Vêtements quelque peu démodés, dans le style des années 1630; remarquer les bottes à éperons, que les officiers d'infanterie portaient également.. **A3** Il est possible que ceci soit le genre de couvre-chef appelé 'Montero', renforcé de bandes de fer. Une armure de corps était encore portée par les piquiers aux environs de 1645, mais devint moins populaire les années suivantes.

**B1** Le rouge était la couleur prédominante, même avant que la New Model Army soit fondée, et devint obligatoire par la suite. Cet officier puritain typique est habillé et équipé sobrement. **B2** Noter la 'cage' aux barreaux exceptionnellement large protégeant la figure, et les deux morceaux métalliques rejoignant les plaques sur les épaules. **B3 et B4** La courte veste ou manteau rouge s'appelle 'cassock'. Des casques de types morion et cabacete se portaient en ce temps-là. Les couleurs de doublures des manteaux variaient, et étaient spéciales pour chaque unité.

**C1** Remarquer les manches déboutonnées sur toute leur longueur, et portées amples; le hausse-col, seul vestige d'armure; et le bâton de commandement remplaçant décorativement le partisan ou halbred habituels. **C2 et C3** Les mousquets plus légers, introduits dans les années 1650, rendirent superflus le repose-mousquet. C3 a un mousquet à silex.

**D1** Les dragons étaient probablement habillés de façon semblable aux mousquetaires de l'infanterie, mais avec des bottes de cheval. **D2 et D3** 'Buff coats' typiques, portés avec des casques découvrant le visage de styles légèrement différents. Cuirasse, sabre et mousqueton à la bretelle. Notez le gantelet de fer, qui protège la main gauche de D3, main qui tient les rênes pendant la bataille.

**E** Les artilleurs ne portaient pas d'uniforme. Les servants du cannon, sans compter les autres soldats qui à l'occasion reçoivent l'ordre de prêter main-forte pour déplacer les pièces pendant la bataille, consistent du cannonier, de son assistant et d'un aide. **E4** est un 'firelock' soldat d'une des compagnies assignées à la garde de l'artillerie pendant la bataille et la marche, et pour cette raison est équipé d'un mousquet à silex—il n'aurait pas été prudent d'avoir des mèches lentes à proximité des tonneaux de poudre.

**F1** Il est de fait qu'avant 1645, deux unités portaient une armure de cuirassier complète, mais on pense qu'elle n'était plus utilisée pour le combat après l'instauration de la 'New Model Army'. Les officiers supérieurs continuèrent peut être à la porter pour les parades, etc.... Ils sont souvent représentés en armure. **F2** Fairfax, joue gauche balafrée en souvenir d'une charge furieuse à Marston Moor, porte encore un autre style de 'buff coat'. Les écharpes cramoisis sont normalement associées avec les royalistes, et les écharpes oranges avec les troupes du parlement, mais nous avons peu d'informations détaillées sur la question. Les officiers supérieurs des deux armées portaient sans aucun doute des écharpes cramoisis occasionnellement. **F3** Remarquer les manches étroites, décorées de cercles de dentelle argentée, attachés au cuir plus lourd du plastron du 'buff coat', décoration à la mode d'alors.

**G1** Monck, le général responsable de la restauration du roi Charles II, est représenté ici dans le style sobre coûtumier aux portraits. Le creux dans la cuirasse est la marque certifiant que le fabricant l'a testée en tirant dessus avant que l'armure ne quitte l'usine. **G2** Sur ce portrait hollandais de Cromwell, peint pendant les années 1650, on le voit portant un costume sobre de velour marron clair. **G3** Un exemple d'habits et d'accessoires plus élaborés: il y avait beaucoup de gentilhommes bien habillés dans les rangs de la 'New Model Army'.

**H** La légende en anglais identifies les drapeaux.

## Farbtafeln

**A1** Es gab keine Vorschriftsuniform, aber wir wissen, dass diese Einheit grüne Kleidung trug, die rot gefüttert war. Eine eiserne Schädelkappe, unter dem Hut getragen, schützt ihn vor Schwertwunden. Er trägt eine Luntenschloss-Muskete, mit flaschenförmigen Behältern für das Pulver an einem Schulterriemen hängend, und eine Musketenstütze. **A2** Ziemlich altmodische Kleidung im Stil der 1630er; und bemerke die gesporrten Stiefel, sogar von Infanterieoffizieren getragen. **A3** Dieser Mützentyp mag als 'montero' bekannt gewesen sein: es ist durch eiserne Streifen verstärkt. Körperrüstung wurde noch von den mit einer Pike bewaffneten Soldaten um ca. 1645 getragen, nahm jedoch in kommenden Jahren an Beliebtheit immer mehr ab.

**B1** Die Hauptuniformfarbe war rot, sogar vor der Gründung der New Model Army, und wurde Vorschrift danach. Dieser Offizier zeigt einen einfachen Kleidungs- und Ausrüstungsstil, typisch für einen Puritaner. **B2** Bemerke den ungewöhnlich grossen 'Korb' aus Stäben, der das Gesicht schützt, und die zwei Stabsätze, die in auf den Schultern liegenden Platten übergehen. **B3 und B4** Die kurze rote Uberjacke oder Mantel wurde 'cassock' genannt. Die Helme beider Typen, morion und cabacete wurden in dieser Periode getragen. Die Farben des Jackenfutters waren verschieden und waren für jede Einheit vorgeschrieben.

**C1** Bemerke die Ärmel, aufgeknöpft entlang ihrer ganzen Länge und lose hängend getragen; der Kragenring, nunmehr als einziges Stück Rüstung getragen; und der 'Fuhrungsstab', eine schmückende Alternative zu den gewöhnlichen partisan oder halberd. **C2, C3** Die leichteren Musketen, eingeführt in den 1650ern, machten die Stützen unnötig; C3 hat eine Steinschloss-Muskete.

**D1** Die Dragoner waren wahrscheinlich sehr ähnlich wie die Infanteriemusketiere angezogen, jedoch mit Reitstiefeln. **D2, D3** Typische 'buff coats', mit gesichtsoffenen Helmen in leicht unterschiedlichen Stilarten, Kürassen, Schwerte und umgeschlungenen Karabinern. Bemerke den 'Zügelhandschuh' aus Eisen, der die linke Hand von D3 schützt, die Hand, die die Zügel in der Schlacht hält.

**E** Die Kanonenmannschaften waren nicht uniformiert. Die direkte Mannschaft, unbeachtend der anderen Männer, denen befohlen worden sein mag, ihre Muskelkraft zum Einsatz zu bringen um die Kanonen in der Schlacht zu verschieben, bestand aus dem Schützen, dem Gehilfen des Schützen und einem Helfer. E4 ist ein 'firelock', ein Soldat von einer der Kompanien, der abkommandiert wurde, die Artillerie in der Schlacht und auf dem Marsch zu bewachen, und war demzufolge mit Steinschloss-Musketen bewaffnet, denn eine brennende Lunte in die Nähe von Pulverfässern zu nehmen, wäre nicht das Gesündeste gewesen.

**F1** Zwei Einheiten waren bekannt, die volle Kürassiersrüstung vor 1645 getragen zu haben, jedoch glaubt man, dass keiner sie nach der Gründung der New Model Army in der Schlacht getragen hat. Höhere Offiziere trugen sie evtl. weiterhin fur Paraden, etc.; sie sind oft darin abgebildet. **F2** Fairfax, dessen linke Wange in einer wütenden Attacke bei Marston Moor verunstaltet wurde, trägt wiederum einen anderen Stil eines 'buff coat'. Karmesinrote Schärpen wurden normalerweise mit den Royalisten und orangefarbene mit den parlamentarischen Truppen in Verbindung gebracht, wir haben jedoch wenig Information über Einzelheiten; höhere Offiziere beider Armeen trugen sicherlich bestickte karmesinrote Schärpen hin und wieder. **F3** Bemerke die dünnen Armel, mit geschlaufter Silberspitze verziert, an dem schwereren Leder befestigt, welches fur den Torso des 'buff coat' benutzt wurde; eine gewöhnliche schmückende Eigenart jener Tage.

**G1** Monck, der General verantwortlich fur die Wiedereinsetzung von König Charles II, trägt hier den ziemlich einfachen Stil, gezeigt in Portraits. Die Einbeulung im Küráss ist das 'Prüfungszeichen', welches zeigt, dass der Hersteller eine Pistolenkugel daraufgefeuert hat, bevor es die Fabrik verliess. **G2** Ein einfacher Anzug aus hellbraunem Samt ist in einem holländischen Portrait von Cromwell, in den 1650ern gemalt, gezeigt. **G3** Ein Beispiel von kunstvollerer Kleidung und Ausrüstung; es gab genug fein angezogene Herren in den Rängen der New Model Army.

**H** Die Fahnen sind in den Titeln der englischen Sprache identifiziert.